Unlikely Heroes

37 INSPIRING STORIES *of* COURAGE *and* HEART *from the* ANIMAL KINGDOM

by

JENNIFER S. HOLLAND

WORKMAN PUBLISHING • NEW YORK

Library of Congress Cataloging-in-Publication Data is available.

ISBN 978-0-7611-7441-7

Design by Raquel Jaramillo and Ariana Abud
Photo research by Melissa Lucier
Photo credits appear on page 246.

Workman books are available at special discounts when purchased in bulk for premiums and sales promotions as well as for fund-raising or educational use. Special editions or book excerpts can also be created to specification. For details, contact the Special Sales Director at the address below, or send an email to specialmarkets@workman.com.

Workman Publishing Company, Inc.
225 Varick Street
New York, NY 10014-4381
workman.com

Printed in the United States of America

First printing October 2014

10 9 8 7 6 5 4 3 2 1

For all those good souls out there giving
neglected animals second chances.
You, too, are heroes.

Jasmine,
"The Giving Greyhound,"
with a new friend.

"A hero is someone who has given his or her life
to something bigger than oneself."
—Joseph Campbell

p. 181

Contents

p. 141

p. 153

p. 17

Joy, sea otter supermom, with a pup.

Introduction

AFTER DARK, WHEN MY BIG DOG, A **KOREAN JINDO**, barks suddenly from his post at the top of the stairs, I thank him with a bear hug (which is apt: I swear he's part polar bear). He's watching out for me. Yes, it's his instinct to guard the home whether I'm in it or not. And, yes, sometimes he barks at the wind. But that doesn't make me less appreciative of his low, menacing *woof*. My Jindo is my hero and all he's had to do to earn that title is to make a little noise on my behalf.

There are certainly bloodier heroics. If you have read *Unlikely Loves*, you may recall the story of Dotty and Stanley, in which a donkey rushed to assist her sheep pal when an out-of-control dog attacked him. There's no question that she put herself at great risk by grabbing the dog in her own jaws and whipping him around— he easily could have turned and laid into her. In the end, Stanley was seriously injured, but Dotty had saved his life.

What's a hero, then? In the human world, that's an easy question to answer. It's the pilot who dies flying the dangerous mission, the guard who takes a bullet for the president, the woman who races into a burning building to rescue a child. Maybe, too, it's the grandma who raises her grandkids for her sick daughter, the man who says no to a promotion to care for his dying dad, the farmer who takes in injured animals and makes them whole again.

And then come heroes that are a bit . . . furrier. My research led me to a wallaby who bounded for help—and pounded its big feet on a door to get it—when a farmer was hit by a falling branch, a pit bull who dragged its injured owner off the train tracks, and an Afghan hound who stubbornly stretched out in front of his owner's riding lawn mower to protect a litter of rabbits in the grass ahead.

In the animal world, I see heroism through a very wide lens. Just as friendship and love can mean this or that, animal heroism can span from here to there. Certainly, those who rush into a dangerous situation to rescue others are heroic. But also, animals who give special care and affection to lonely or injured creatures are heroic. Animals who act as surrogates for nonrelated animals, and thereby work toward the conservation of other species, have a heroic streak (even if they don't realize their own generosity). Animals like service dogs who spend their lives supporting people in need—these are amazingly valiant creatures. Even if they are trained to do so, I still give them "hero" credit for all the giving.

Not all would agree. A writer I know, Cat Warren, author of the wonderfully interesting *What the Dog Knows*, works with cadaver dogs—dogs that help find human remains. In her book, she mentions that she once sighed aloud that her dog was her hero and immediately regretted it. "I was tired, and I shouldn't have said it, even though at that moment, I meant it," she wrote. She said handlers who see true heroism in working animals have been "made mindless by the fantasy that their dogs are infallible—and could solve complex puzzles by themselves. . . . Humans need to set dogs up for success."

She's right, of course. In the case of working animals, trainers and owners play a vital role, and at least for those folks, that's important to remember. Still, her instinct to call her dog heroic reveals something about people: We like to see bravery and generosity in nonpeople. It's comforting. It gives us a warm, fuzzy feeling in an often gloomy world.

Helpful behavior is seen throughout the animal kingdom, and the rewards to the giver aren't always clear. Consider that common chimpanzees, once thought to be only "reluctant altruists" (giving only under pressure), have now been shown to prefer what's called prosocial behavior to selfish behavior. That's a fancy way of saying they may choose to do nice things for others when they stand to gain nothing obvious. In one study, adult female chimps decided to share food with "friends" who weren't dominant over or related to them. Rats will do the same thing for their

Lon Hodge and Gander.

buddies, as will numerous other mammals.

Bonobo chimpanzees are especially generous to others of their group. I'll skip the explicit details—this is a family book, after all—but let's just say everyone "gives affection" to everyone else—often and out in the open. In bonobo society, loving one another is a way to keep the peace. Certainly, an individual enjoys the affection, but the benefits go in all directions.

Here's an unlikely giver: the vampire bat. I observed these strange little mammals recently, along with Gerry Carter, a student at the University of Maryland who is trying to understand the bats' motives for sharing food outside the family. He's studying a hormone, oxytocin, that may be partly responsible for the generosity. In a darkened lab, peering through video cameras that zoom in nice and close, we watched as one bat gave a mouthful of blood (yes, they really do eat blood) not just to a hungry relative, but also to an unrelated bat who came begging. (They beg by licking each other's mouths—very intimate.)

As with the chimps, this is one of those "helping" behaviors that doesn't at first glance make evolutionary sense—why waste energy and food on an animal that doesn't share your DNA? Isn't the need to spread genes what it's all about? But Gerry points out that a social bond among bats has value beyond merely helping relatives survive.

To make this easier to understand, "Think of human friendship," he says. "We make many small sacrifices to help friends in need, but maintaining such friendships is important for our own well-being." If we limited our friendships to family, he says, we would be limiting our own social support network—those who may be companions now and can help us down the line.

The same is likely true of the bats. And just like when you help a human friend, a bat's generosity isn't a strategic act with the expectation of repayment. Some bats are givers, just as some people are. There can be a real desire to be nice.

Here's another way to think about it. "A mother's love is real. But also, loving moms have more surviving children," says Gerry. That love, then, is in the DNA; the genetic and emotional ties are intertwined. The same goes for bats: Over evolutionary time, Gerry says, those that freely fed others were better able to survive and make babies. So, feeding nonkin actually does make sense, on all levels.

Even honeybees make what seem to be sacrifices for others. A recent study showed that worker bees continue to defend and bring food to the colony even when the hive is collapsing and soon to be defunct. Instead of becoming selfish, *looking out for number one*, the bees—who are all related—work toward the greater good. Each gives to the family—to keep the family genes going—even if it means that bee dies in the process.

If you want some fancy terms for all this, biologists call the behavior in bees *evolutionary altruism*—the bees as a whole will do better than the individual "generous" bee. In the case of a chimp sharing food, that's *behavioral altruism*, meaning in the short term the giver loses out (gives up food) but there might be benefits later (the friend might share *her* food). The chimp isn't necessarily thinking ahead to that day. Still, she wins in the end.

And finally, there's *psychological altruism*, when there aren't selfish interests involved at all—just the drive to help another out of empathy. Just recently scientists showed that Asian elephants (like great apes, dogs, and ravens) will console a distressed herd mate with caresses and soothing chirping sounds. I believe most mammals have such capacity. Isn't it lovely to think that creatures besides humans do nice things simply out of the goodness of their hearts?

Here's an unsurprising outcome: There are lots of dogs in this volume! In fact, I had to squeeze out some great dog stories—rescues from the rubble, heroics on the battlefield, lifesaving leaps from helicopters to pluck people from the ocean—to make room for nondogs. Happily, though, my research uncovered a whole host of creatures saving the lives of others or working hard to enrich those lives. Llamas. A camel. Sheep. Rabbits. Gorillas. Horses. An elk. An elephant seal! They're all here.

One thing I love about animal heroes is their modesty (for lack of a better word). Animals who act generously don't care about recognition, about TV coverage or awards. The good-deed doer, his good deed done, goes back to whatever he was doing before the incident. Eating. Sleeping. Pooping. Rolling in the mud. Not thinking about his valor. Not bragging to others about his brave deed. Just *being*.

And that's a true hero in my book.

Superheroes

Spontaneous Acts of Bravery

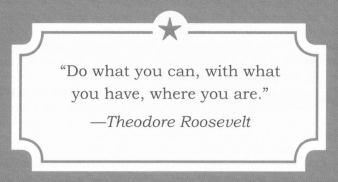

> "Do what you can, with what
> you have, where you are."
>
> —*Theodore Roosevelt*

HERE ARE THE TRUE CHAMPIONS OF THE ANIMAL WORLD, the creatures who have swooped in, set aside fear, and faced danger in service of another. Whether they know it or not, they are courageous. Their quick acts have saved lives.

Lincoln
the Lionhearted
Leonberger

L INCOLN WAS A LION. OR MIGHT AS WELL HAVE BEEN. The Leonberger, Lincoln's breed, is a proud giant among dogs, a king among canines. Leos can fill out to as much as 200 pounds. But their furry faces, grace, and gentle nature belie their immense power—and this was especially true of Lincoln. Though he reached 157 pounds, his sweet demeanor was even larger, as was his devotion to his owner, Vic Neumann. "My wife called him my Velcro dog because he was always with me, stuck to my side," Vic says.

Vic and his wife, Joan, of Avon, Connecticut, had two Leos before Lincoln arrived, but one had recently died. After eleven years as part of a pair, Mia, the other, was heartbroken over the loss.

She seemed to shrink in her sadness, her boisterousness crushed, and nothing the couple did eased her pain. They rescued Lincoln in part to give Mia a friend. It took a few encounters, but once the dogs started playing, "Mia sparked right up; we could see her change in attitude," Vic says. "With him around, Mia's personality came back. He was her big little brother, and they truly fell in love."

And when age began to slow Mia down, Vic and Joan rescued yet another Leo, this one from a puppy mill. Despite starting out in a rough place, Cassie fit right in with the others, making it a family of five—three furry giants and two loving owners.

One Saturday in the summer of 2009, after two weeks of heavy rain, Vic, Lincoln, and Cassie were all eager to stretch their legs, so the threesome headed for the Farmington River. Their favorite spot was nearby and Vic had been visiting it for some eighteen years, dogs always in tow. The river was running 13 feet above normal and lapping over the bank, but Leonbergers are strong swimmers; they even have webbed feet. In Italy, they are used to rescue people at sea, lowered from helicopters into the water. So Vic wasn't worried about them going for a swim. "I stood at the edge of the water and threw a stick, and they raced to get it, play-fighting over it, as people there cheered them on," he recalls.

Cassie had always been an eager water dog, sometimes paddling the 50 yards across to the river's far bank. But on this day, as she reached the middle of the river, she seemed to struggle. The water was moving fast, and "she was working hard but not making any progress," Vic says. "My friend Roger was there, too, and I told him I was worried. Then it occurred to me, when I saw uprooted trees floating fast, that one of her legs might be stuck in some debris beneath the water."

"I have to go in after her," Vic told Roger, giving the man his cell phone. Then Vic slogged into the river, still wearing his work boots and jeans.

He didn't get far before the river took control. "The water just picked me up and carried me away. I was being moved at a very rapid pace north, downstream, toward where the Farmington empties into the Connecticut River, and away from Cassie." Vic was still recovering from a recent shoulder surgery, and had done some serious brush cutting that morning, so pain and weakness set in quickly. Still, "at first I wasn't worried for me as much as for the dog. How was I going to get to her now? But then I felt that helpless fear, realizing I couldn't keep myself afloat." Vic was dog-paddling but couldn't stop himself from being pulled under. "When I took my first gulp of water, I really thought, this is it."

AWARDS & HONORS

In 2010, Lincoln was elected to the Leonberger Club of America Hall of Fame as an "Outstanding Canine Good Citizen."

Vic began to panic as the current carried him around a bend, out of sight of the people on shore. Now it was just man and river, and the river was poised to win.

"That's when I heard a huffing behind me, a blowing sound, and at first I wasn't sure what it was," says Vic. "Then I realized it was Lincoln. He appeared as if out of nowhere, and like a missile he shot up under my arm, literally lifting my whole torso out of the water." Vic wrapped his arms around the animal's massive neck, his life preserver, and held on. "I was worried I'd drag him under, but he was strong. I looked for something to aim for and said, 'Swim, Lincoln!' He did. I steered us toward a tree that had washed off the bank, and when he got me there I grabbed onto a branch."

Vic was holding Lincoln's collar in one hand and the branch in the other, when he heard his friend Roger, who had leaped in after Vic, nearly fly by. Vic grabbed his friend's T-shirt before the stream could ferry him away. "Pretty soon we're all clinging to the tree a half mile away from where the people were. We were there for about forty-five minutes, yelling for help."

Finally, a couple kayaking nearby heard the cries and came to assist. They had ropes in their boat and were able to pull the two men and the dog back to the riverbank. "When we got to where we'd started, there was Cassie," says Vic. "I cried for joy when I saw her." She had been rescued, too—by a high school kid, a swimmer, who happened to be at the river that day. He'd dived down and released the dog's legs, which were indeed caught on some twisted limbs and rocks under the water. "She was standing there looking at me as if to say, Why did you go off swimming without me?" Vic recalls.

Vic nearly collapsed in relief, seeing Cassie's rapidly wagging tail. "My emotions poured out of me. I offered the boy a reward for his selfless act of heroism and the next school day called his school, in a neighboring town, to let them know what a fine thing he had done."

Lincoln the lifeguard, on the riverbank.

Witnesses told Vic that as soon as he'd been swept off his feet, Lincoln jumped in to chase him. "He may have been swimming behind me all along, then when he saw things got really bad, he lifted me up." Vic wonders whether Lincoln was torn between whether to follow Vic or try to help his pal Cassie. "But he came after me. He saved my life."

The hero dog got plenty of attention once Vic's story got out; a media frenzy followed, including special awards and a segment in an Animal Planet film reenacting the event. And in 2011, after Lincoln passed away, letters and emails flooded in to honor him, with words that Vic continues to cherish. From those notes: "Lincoln was a beautiful soul, a beautiful boy. In celebrating his life, we can all silently thank him for yours, too. He was a force of nature, and his strong and gentle spirit will endure."

A youthful Gimpy.

The Elephant Seal *Who* Battled Bullies

THE FIRST THING I NOTICED WAS THE SMELL. I HAD been scaling the rocks bordering a California beach in hopes of getting a good view, but here my eyes were secondary. The musky wet-dog-meets-fish-breath odor hit me like a wall. Elephant seals. I crouched down a respectful distance away, ignoring the stink and loving the scene: dozens of massive lumps of brownish-gray flesh strewn about in the sand like . . . well . . . beached whales.

These loud, smelly pinnipeds—the marine mammal group that includes seals, sea lions, and walruses—must be some of the most gregarious and animated of sea creatures. During mating season, they form a colony that recalls a fraternity party. With females seeming to ignore them entirely, the males wave

At the time of the attack, Gimpy outweighed each pup by 200 pounds.

their large, floppy, trunklike snouts proudly in the air as they trumpet their dominance over the rest of the raucous herd. The biggest can weigh as much as 4,000 pounds and stretch to 14 feet, and they'll attack or at least charge any competitors or interlopers in their midst. Females with young are also particularly ornery when strangers tread too near. (I was directed by a park ranger to stay well back.)

Fortunately for Hugh Ryono, the elephant seals that came after him one sunny day in 1995 were just a year old, nowhere near their adult size and attitude. Still, "they were teething and in the stage in which they fight to establish hierarchy," Hugh recalls. "They had very effective canine teeth that, on unprotected human flesh, would cause serious puncture and rake wounds." Hugh might have ended up torn and bloody that day. But he escaped unscathed because of an unlikely protector named Gimpy.

Gimpy (hardly a hero's name, but don't let that fool you) was a young elephant seal who had come to the Marine Mammal Care Center at Fort MacArthur, in San Pedro, California, the year before with a head trauma that paralyzed her left side and caused partial blindness. The poor thing seemed unlikely to recover. She managed to heal somewhat, but the staff knew she'd never be able to survive in the wild again. As a volunteer at the center, Hugh spent a lot of time feeding the young seal and cleaning her pen, and he was pleasantly surprised that she showed him no aggression. In fact, he guessed she might even like having him around.

Gimpy's roommates were less cordial. On that potentially bloody day, Hugh had entered the seal pen alone to clean up after the half-dozen smaller but very rambunctious pups. He held a crowding board between himself and the seals in case they turned aggressive. But while moving around the wet, slick space, he slipped on a sardine and flopped to the ground, dropping his shield.

He landed hard enough to see stars, and what happened next seemed to be in slow motion, he says. "Dazed, I looked up to see three angry seals approaching," he wrote in his blog after the event. "Each seemed to be intent on trying out their new canines on me!" The yelping seals

Elephant seal pups, though cute, can be very aggressive.

cruised right over his board, keeping him from grabbing it, and headed straight for him.

Out of the corner of his eye, Hugh glimpsed another mass of blubber, a particularly big one, moving in. He assumed his attackers had fanned out and he'd be jumped from all sides. He knew he was in for a rough afternoon.

But that 300 pounds of flesh to his right wasn't in on the attack. It . . . she . . . was coming to Hugh's rescue. It was Gimpy.

Perhaps his head was still spinning from the fall, but, he says, "She looked almost angelic coming toward me." Once she was beside him, he managed to get on hands and knees and crawl over her body, putting her between him and his attackers. The seal was unfazed by the physical contact. And when the feisty adolescents continued to bear down on them, she gave them a silent, openmouthed warning, head bobbing up and down, teeth prominently displayed, that ended the seals' charge. Threatened by the bigger animal (she outweighed each by some 200 pounds), they began to back off, and Hugh was able to scramble for his board, ending his immediate danger.

Hugh still had work to do, so rather than dwell on what had just happened, he brushed himself off, patted his rescuer on the back, and said,

Gimpy gets a bath.

simply, "Thanks, Gimpy." Later, he gave the seal an extra fish as a thank-you treat, thinking how it was hardly enough of a reward for such a great deed. Because of Gimpy, Hugh knew, he'd avoided a real mauling.

Hugh's experience, he says, made him look at the animals he worked with as true individuals. "They're not just components of a herd or flock or pod. Each has its own personality and spirit."

So why did Gimpy lumber to Hugh's rescue that day, putting herself in front of an angry mob? "She wasn't a fighter. She was essentially blind and had a distinct disadvantage in a fight." So it wasn't her nature to intervene. Her openmouthed threat "was all a facade," says Hugh. "She's a gentle giant!

"But during her early struggles to survive," Hugh says, "I used to be her lifeguard, helping her out of the pool." (The seal's early injuries had affected her coordination.) "She'd then lie there blowing bubbles and I'd have one-way conversations with her, talking about this and that, about things I couldn't really discuss with anyone else." Gimpy was a good listener; she never interrupted!

"I think she got used to my voice," he says. "So when she heard me yell as I slipped in the pen, she came to see if I was okay. To me, she became a real hero that day."

The Horse Who Fought the Ferocious Dog

SUNNY BOY WAS UNBREAKABLE. HE WAS A HORSE WHO knew nothing but how to fear, and that had turned him against the human world. He'd had multiple owners, and at least one of them had been very mean to him. He was slapped around, even beaten with a pipe. Now no one could get close to him. "There's a time in an animal's life, soon after birth, that it imprints and bonds with its mother," says Mark Wendell. "I don't think this horse ever had that connection—with anyone or anything."

That is, until Mark's daughter, Chloe, showed up. Sunny Boy was already six years old and had no social skills. He seemed mentally out of reach. "His owners at the time pretty much said, if you can catch him, he's yours" (for a price, of course). Chloe was determined. She quickly fell in love with him, but she instinctively understood the horse would not accept immediate affection. Instead of chasing him, she let him come to her. And very soon, he was approaching her and letting her touch him. Shortly thereafter, she was on his back. "I spent the time he needed, let him learn I wasn't going to hurt him," she says. "And then we just bonded."

Horses are part of the Wendell family culture. Mark got his first horse for his first birthday. He gave the same gift to his eldest daughter and watched with pride as she grew up to be a talented rider and trainer. And with Sunny Boy, she met the extra challenge of mending a horse who was mentally shattered.

Though troubled, he was (and still is) a real beauty. "Like something out of a fairy tale," says Mark, "a golden palomino, nicely built, with a beautiful head. If he's in a group of horses, you definitely notice him first."

So, Sunny Boy was right where he belonged one beautiful spring day, lined up and looking dashing for a parade in Vivian, Louisiana, a tiny town known for its annual Redbud Festival. Mark and Chloe had been in the parade before, and Chloe's sister, Kristen Burgess, then thirteen, was a new rider. The trio was up with the sun, saddling up for the big event, and dressed in their best Western gear.

As the festivities began, things went awry for the family. "We had just turned onto the main road that goes through the middle of town, when suddenly a dog came racing toward us," Chloe recalls. It was a pit bull and not a sweet one. She says she had noticed the dog earlier, barking in the back of a pickup truck, but had assumed its owner would tie it up before the parade began.

"But the dog was loose, and he was on the attack," Chloe says. "He ran directly toward my sister's horse, Angel. He actually ran into her and almost knocked the horse over! That's not easy to do—Angel is a big animal."

The dog began assaulting the horse from underneath, biting her stomach, and the bigger animal danced around, trying, and failing, to get away from the dog.

"My sister didn't know what to do," Chloe says, "so she was just holding on tight. But then her horse stumbled off the road into a rocky patch, so she decided it was safest to jump off." Worried for her sister on the ground, Chloe, too, dismounted and ran toward the action. "That's when the dog turned and focused on us," she says.

PIT BULL REPUTE

Before they got branded as a dangerous breed, pit bulls were considered ideal pets, because they are so good with people. In truth, no breed is either gentle or vicious. Studies show that the owner can be more influential than a dog's DNA.

Then Sonny Boy did something astounding. Instead of turning tail and running, which is the characteristic behavior of a horse (especially a nervous one), he ran right to his owner and put himself between Chloe and the dog. "He actually knocked me back out of the way," she says, "and then he kicked the dog in the face!" Although the kick didn't stop the dog fully, it did turn him away long enough for Chloe and Kristen to scramble out of danger.

Mark's horse was the next to be attacked. The girls' dad had been down the street when the dog showed up, and he and a friend came galloping over as soon as they saw the commotion. Their kicks to the dog were also fruitless. And then the crazed canine turned his attention to Mark's horse and latched on to its leg, gripping tightly even as the horse started to run. The horse actually dragged the mad dog down the street a ways.

Finally a police officer got control of the dog, but plenty of damage had been done. Mark's horse was terribly traumatized. As for the others, it took a lot of stitches to put them back together. Sunny Boy had pulled a ligament in one leg; he never fully healed. "He limps a little still and we don't ride him much," Mark says. "But his personality is still the same. He's ornery and doesn't like to be caught. Except by Chloe, of course."

It's still hard for the family to believe what Sunny Boy did that day. Horses are flight animals, Mark explains. "If there's a stressful situation, they want to get away. That's just how they are. If I hadn't seen what happened for myself, I might not have believed it." He said a woman who also witnessed it came up to him later to marvel at what she'd seen. "She said she'd thought it was a figment of her imagination. It was such unexpected behavior. He saved my daughter's life."

And Sunny Boy, ornery as he may be at times, keeps on giving. Mark works with ex-convicts and troubled kids, and the family horses are used in counseling sessions. In this program, too, Sunny Boy has a special role to play. "We use him as an example to people who have been traumatized in their lives—kids who have been abused and such," says Mark. "He shows people that even when you've faced adversity, you can do well in life, even be a hero. Very few animals can teach that lesson."

Common dolphins like these protected Robbie and his students.

The Lifeguarding Dolphins

LET ME START OUT WITH A LITTLE PRO-SHARK MESSAGE before dipping into a scary shark story. Sharks are incredible, stunning, and awe-inspiring animals. Typically they're not interested in humans, and only rarely do they kill people—no more often than do large animals on land (think elephants and hippos). Many times, if a shark bites a person, it then lets go—as if realizing it made a mistake.

But sharks are predators and they aren't shy about it. And sadly, there are cases of human versus beast that end badly.

New Zealand's waters house lots of hot spots for these marine predators. Aware of the potential danger, New Zealander Robbie Howes was taking great care back in 2004 as he led a small group of new lifeguards from the Whangarei Heads Surf Lifesaving Patrol at Ocean Beach on a long ocean swim—to improve their strength and build their confidence. They were about 330 feet offshore and planned to swim just over half a mile, from one end of the beach to the other.

Robbie's daughter, Nicky, then fifteen, was one of the student lifeguards, along with two of her good friends, Karina and Helen. The group started out together, moving at a good pace, but before they could get far, they realized they had company.

"The fin came out of nowhere, and the girls panicked for a moment, but I quickly worked out it was a dolphin," recalls Robbie. It turned out that it wasn't just one animal but a whole pod. They surrounded the swimmers and moved along with them as if part of the team. Although not an everyday occurrence, "we'd certainly swum with dolphins before. We often interact with them," Robbie says. So there was no reason to be surprised or afraid.

But about 20 minutes into the joint swim, Robbie recalls, something strange happened. "The dolphins' behavior changed. They started packing in very tight around us and then hammering the water with their tails. They were quite close to us—we could have reached out and touched them—as they hammered away, splashing." The swimmers felt the dolphins' agitation and wondered what was going on.

Robbie decided to move away from the circle to try to figure out what was upsetting the dolphins, so he kicked hard and

Robbie Howes, the lucky lifeguard.

managed to separate himself, swimming off about 30 feet. Helen, wanting to stay with her instructor, decided to go with him.

The largest dolphin in the pod broke from the rest and swam straight for Robbie and Helen. It dove down right in front of them and Robbie turned his body to see where it would emerge. "That's when I saw a dark shape in the water arcing around us, fast, at ninety degrees to the dolphin," he says. "My whole body contracted in some sort of primal defense mode as I realized what it was."

It was a 10-foot great white shark.

Robbie saw right away that the dolphin's maneuver had kept them from being attacked by this predator, and had also put the dolphin at risk. "My guess is that the shark saw we were vulnerable and was taking the opportunity to come after us. And the dolphin figured out what was happening and dove in front of us to divert the shark from its course."

But the predator wasn't quite finished with its rounds. And with just his head and shoulders above the water's surface, Robbie couldn't follow the shark's movements for more than a couple of seconds. That was long enough, though, to know it was heading toward his daughter and Karina. "It was one of those situations where time seemed to stand still," he says. Before he could react, "the dolphins around Nicky and Karina went ballistic, spinning and splashing and beating their tails. And then, suddenly, everything died down. They'd scared the shark away. It was gone."

At this point, Robbie was the only person in the group who knew that the great white had paid a visit. People on the beach who had seen the activity thought the swimmers were frolicking and playing with the dolphins, not having a near miss with a shark. He saw no reason to scare the others, so as the group traveled back to the beach, he kept the news to himself.

It turns out that dolphins naturally "ball up" in a tight group as a defense mechanism, and the tail-slapping is a warning sign to approaching predators. "These were telltale signs that a shark was about," Robbie says. "I guess if we'd known that, we might

GREAT WHITE SHARK

Adult great whites can swim more than 40 miles per hour. Unlike other fish, sharks don't have swim bladders to help them float. Instead, their large livers, filled with fats and oils, give them buoyancy and keep them from being bottom dwellers.

have realized sooner that we were in danger." But maybe they were better off not knowing, he says. "We might have reacted badly, trying to swim to shore, splitting up. This way the dolphins kept us together" and did the work of scaring the predator away. And though the dolphins were acting naturally, Robbie felt that they were deliberately including the swimmers in their circle, keeping them safe. Certainly the breakaway dolphin had chosen to help.

Robbie didn't tell his students the truth until the next morning, "after they were back in the water," he says. No doubt every passing dark patch was anxiously scrutinized that day.

Before the big reveal, "I had no idea," Nicky admits. "My friend and I just thought the dolphins were crazy. We were so caught up in their behavior that we didn't know anything about the shark. I would have been so scared if I'd known."

Why did the dolphins intervene on the swimmers' behalf? Robbie suggests it's because of positive past experience with people. "These pods are regular visitors to Ocean Beach. They interact with us playfully, but we also respect their space, and we don't pester them. Maybe they see us as extended family of sorts."

Says Nicky, "It definitely helps to know they're out there."

The Cat *Who* Faced Fire

A VERY SPECIAL MOM PASSED AWAY IN **2008.** HER NAME was Scarlett and her death brought scores of people around the world to tears. In New York, she was given a hero's farewell, her face lighting up the Jumbotron above Times Square. But who was she?

Scarlett seemed to be just your standard kitty cat—a young female calico who was, in 1996, homeless in New York City, just trying to make her way. Her fame came after an extraordinary act of compassion that made news across the globe.

She had been nobody's cat for some time, and had recently given birth to a litter of five in an abandoned garage in Brooklyn. The new mother was inside with her four-week-old babies on

March 30, 1996, when the building went up in flames. An FDNY firefighter named David Giannelli, who would be a part of the teams that responded to the 9/11 tragedy years later, had a soft spot for animals. He's the one who first discovered the kittens all lined up in the grass away from the flames. He realized quickly that the mother must have placed them

there, one by one, going back into the building time after time to pluck each by the scruff of its neck and carry it to safety. When he found the mom, she was burned badly—her fur was singed off, leaving ugly welted skin beneath, and her eyes and ears were bare and blistered—but that hadn't stopped her from continuing her rescue. She saved all five of her babies.

Karen Wellen of New York adopted Scarlett a few months after the incident, and proudly cared for her for the next twelve years. "I'd seen on a TV report that the animal shelter was looking for just the right person to adopt her if she survived," Karen says. "I had lost my twenty-two-year-old cat not long before, so it would be a very special animal to take that spot in my life." Also, Karen had recently been in a bad car wreck, and felt "less than perfect" herself. She liked the idea of rescuing an animal who shared her pain. This was definitely the cat for the job. After much consideration and even personal interviews, the shelter chose Karen to do the honors.

She says that one of the kittens eventually died from its injuries, but the others were adopted in pairs soon after the fire. Scarlett, meanwhile, settled into her new home easily. Karen says, "She was incredibly smart and gentle. She had a lot of scarring and sensitive skin, and had lost her outer eyelids, so she needed a special cream put in her eyes three times a day. But you wouldn't have known from her personality what she'd endured." Even later, when the cat became ill with lymphoma and kidney problems, her sweet temperament remained.

Scarlett and her kittens.

"She was my guru, my teacher," Karen says, "something you need living in New York, where we have a tendency to lose our tempers. She was so calm, always loving and snuggling and purring. A great influence."

And she really was a hero, Karen believes, "not just because of what she did but also how she lived her life. She didn't let what she'd gone through affect her. She kept a positive outlook—if one can say that about a cat—never complaining. Scarlett was always playing and jumping, running around the dining room table trying to catch your leg. This animal was fully engaged in life."

When you think about it, maybe it was wonderfully natural that Scarlett did what she did. Mothers are programmed to protect their children. In most mammals, anyway, the maternal instinct can easily override mere logic. It gives moms the strength and bravery to do things they would otherwise avoid, including facing danger.

Still, it's amazing the way this one cat's heart, or something intrinsically linked to it, must have blocked what her brain was telling her. She did what she had to do, paid the price, and then pushed on.

Scarlett never let her pain or scars stop her from playing.

Pushing a wildebeest calf to safety as a croc and zebra stand by.

The
Valiant Hippo
at the River

IN THE WILDERNESS OF AFRICA'S SERENGETI, WHEN THE ground begins to scorch and crack under a relentless sun, the mammals get moving. From June to October, the 12,000-square-mile stretch in northern Tanzania and southwestern Kenya is no place to be. Water dries up, and food is scarce. To survive, animals like wildebeests, zebras, and Thomson's gazelles—about 2 million total—take a very long walk north toward greener pastures.

They head to the still-lush Masai Mara, where they'll munch on grasses for four months, until it rains again back home and they can return to the Serengeti. From a distance, the migration is majestic, the giant herds moving en masse across a vast expanse. But down on the ground, the reality can be harrowing.

For wildebeests, crossing the river can be a scary undertaking.

At the Mara River, perhaps the hardest part of the journey, lives hang in the balance. Deep and fast moving when the animals arrive, the water is an obstacle in itself. But it is made extra deadly by crocodiles. The reptiles lie in wait for the herds, to fatten up on the weary ungulates. Their strategy is to hone in on the small and the weak that falter in the current. Many migrants never reach the far bank.

One particular June, Abdul Karim, a resident Masai Mara

naturalist and the head guide for a safari camp called Sanctuary Olonana, had been watching wildebeests and zebras progress together toward the river and knew it was nearly time for their crossing. "They were massing toward a narrow spot we call Kaburu, which means 'dangerous' in local Swahili slang. The river was high after heavy rains and there were so many animals—I knew they would have to keep moving."

He was right. "When they start to cross, it's like a stampede," he says. "Everyone is desperate to get to the other side without getting eaten by the hungry crocodiles or swept away by the strong river current." Abdul positioned his Jeep so the tourists he was leading could see the animals struggle from bank to bank. There were hippos on shore, the group noticed, territorial beasts that aren't afraid to attack another animal that gets in their way. But on this day, they stood back, letting the frantic herds splash into the danger zone.

It was madness. Crocodiles lunged at some animals. Others lost their footing and slipped beneath the surface. The water rushed, the dying animals called out in anguish. The lucky ones clambered up onto dry land. "It went on for about two hours, with so many drowning in the chaos," Abdul says.

Then came an unbelievable event. "The hippos had stayed at a distance until the last ten or so wildebeests were crossing," Abdul says. "In the middle of the group, a female and her calf were following closely." As the mother plunged into the water, the calf remained at her heels, trying desperately to keep up. "The mother, being stronger, managed the current and climbed the steep riverbank before turning to look back," Abdul says. "But her calf was getting washed away. It was adrift, struggling and running out of air." It seemed to try to turn back, but its strength was sapped. The watchers knew that if a croc didn't nab it, the calf would soon drown anyway.

That's when one of the hippos made a move. And not the move you might expect.

"This large hippo, which turned out to be a female, went into the water and headed straight for the struggling calf. She nudged it, pushing it toward the bank, where the mother wildebeest was making frantic runs up and back." The baby scrambled onto land and ran to its mother, resting briefly against her before starting to suckle. Abdul and his group couldn't help but applaud. "We all expected the hippo to tear the poor calf to bits. But that's not what happened at all."

Meanwhile, other animals were still entering the

The heroic hippo in action!

water. Then, the current grabbed up a zebra foal like it had the young wildebeest just before. As the baby flailed about, its hind legs stuck between rocks, our unlikely hero offered her services once again, supporting the zebra from behind until its hooves met the land. "It panted there a bit," says Abdul, "then started a wobbly walk to its mother, who I'm sure had almost given up hope."

SWEATY HIPPOS

To protect their bare skin, which is exposed to strong sunlight much of the time, hippos produce "supersweat," a red filmy substance that acts as sunscreen, insect repellent, and antibiotic, all in one.

It turned out that the helpful hippo was a lactating mom herself, her own baby within view along with the rest of her family. It was her motherly instinct, Abdul suggests, that compelled her to assist the vulnerable calves. "But it was truly heroic the way she crossed species boundaries," he says. A hippo, of all things—an animal not known for its tolerance of others—had spent precious energy saving two babies not her own.

Says Abdul, "Let that be a lesson to the human race!"

Binti Jua.

Two Good-Gorilla Tales

BINTI JUA

Around lunchtime on a summer day in August 1996, a little boy visiting the Brookfield Zoo near Chicago, Illinois, eager to see big animals up close, climbed up where he shouldn't have gone. He lost his footing and somersaulted over the barrier, falling some 20 feet down into the gorilla habitat.

Craig Demitros, then a lead zookeeper and now curator of primates, was having lunch just outside the exhibit. He knew something bad had happened when he heard people yelling and saw frantic families pushing through the emergency exit. He was soon announcing a "signal 13"—a potentially life-threatening situation.

The boy was lying unconscious on the floor of the exhibit while chaos erupted above. Then one of the gorillas, an eight-year-old female named Binti Jua, approached the motionless body. By the time Craig and two colleagues looked over the edge of the wall, "Binti was below us with her seventeen-month-old baby on her back and a three-year-old human boy draped over her right arm."

Zoo staff worked at lightning speed, using water hoses to herd the rest of the gorillas away from the boy and into their night quarters. Meanwhile, Binti carried the motionless bundle about 75 feet, across a stream and to a log away from the other animals. At one point, her back to the other animals, she seemed to rock the child back and forth like a mother would a sleeping baby. Finally, she set him down. And then she joined her gorilla kin as they moved inside.

Binti Jua cradles the injured boy.

The boy began to regain consciousness after Binti left, and zoo staff, along with paramedics who happened to be near, descended, stabilized him on an emergency backboard, carried him out of the exhibit, and loaded him into a zoo ambulance. Within 20 minutes after the fall, the boy was delivered to a nearby hospital. "It felt like it took hours," Craig says. "I was amazed when I found out how fast it all happened."

Was Binti a hero? Some say absolutely. Others are more careful about a label that suggests a purposeful action. "We can only speculate about her motivation," Craig says. She was the closest one to the fallen child and, "honestly, if someone dropped a backpack, a water bottle, a cell phone, any object, over the wall, she or another gorilla might have gone to pick it up just out of curiosity. Was she actually trying to protect the boy from the other gorillas? We just don't know." It turned out the boy only had a broken wrist and some cuts and bruises, so certainly Binti's actions caused no extra damage. "Fortunately, she was gentle with him when she carried him around," Craig says.

And Binti, of course, may have been doing "the right thing" consciously or naturally. She'd been hand-raised, so she was very used to people. She'd even had some maternal training by her keepers, since she didn't have the role models she would have learned from in a gorilla family group in the wild. "The fact that she had her own baby also might be a factor," Craig says. It was fortunate that the child was unconscious, he points out. If he'd been crying and flailing about, Binti might have seen him as a threat. And if a more aggressive gorilla had been the one to handle the child, things could have gone very, very badly. "We were lucky in so many ways that day," Craig says.

Binti Jua's name is Swahili, and means "Daughter of Sunshine" (her father was Sunshine), which somehow seems appropriate for an animal that gave many sunny days to a child who might otherwise have missed out. That child, now a man and long recovered from his fall, has remained out of the public eye. His name was never reported and the zoo protected his identity and his story. (They also copyrighted Binti Jua's name to keep others from exploiting it for profit.) "We believe he returned to the zoo a few times after this happened," Craig says, "but anonymously."

In addition to the happy outcome of the gorilla's actions that day, the incident provided the zoo with a rapt audience eager to be educated about gorillas. "Some people have this King Kong image of gorillas," says Sondra Katzen of the zoo's public affairs office. "We've been working hard to change that." Gorillas are actually highly intelligent, very social, and mainly gentle within their own groups.

Three generations of Binti Jua's family now share the Brookfield exhibit, and she has risen from the position of awkward youngster to unlikely hero to matriarch, her daughter and granddaughter by her side. The zoo plans to breed her again soon. We can only hope her next baby is just like her.

JAMBO

Long before Binti Jua did her good deed, another gorilla was making headlines. On a Sunday afternoon in 1986, at the Durell Wild-

Jambo watches onlookers from his post between his family and the fallen boy.

life Park (then the Jersey Zoo) in the Channel Islands off England, the gorilla complex was packed with onlookers. No surprise there: Watching gorillas feels a bit like peering into the window of a human household, with a grumpy grandpa slouched in a chair and unruly kids battling for adult attention.

Brian Le Lion was there, a teen hanging out with his mom, dad, and little brother. He had a video camera on his shoulder and was enjoying capturing the day, and the animals, on film. The family was heading toward the gorilla complex when they heard shouting from that direction.

"When we got over there, we saw there was a crowd, and there was a five-year-old boy over the wall, maybe fifteen feet down, inside the animals' concrete enclosure," Brian recalls. The boy had fallen out of his father's grasp as the father held him up for a better look.

Inspecting the child.

Then came Jambo. A powerhouse who could send a child fly-ing with a swing of his furry arm, the top gorilla of the zoo's group strolled into view. "It was gradual, his approach, but he moved closer and closer to the boy—with a female and youngsters follow-ing," recalls Brian. When Jambo reached the unconscious boy, he stopped and looked at him intently. "Jambo didn't touch him right then, but he was curious about this creature in his space. He leaned in close. Eventually he touched his back lightly, very gen-tly, and then smelled his hand, as if checking the boy's scent." The gorilla then glanced up at the crowd above. Meanwhile, the female and young apes decided to take a closer look at Jambo's prize.

"That could have been really dangerous, if the animals got all riled up over the boy," Brian said. "But Jambo saved the day. He got between them and the boy, as if he was protecting him. I'm not sure what he was telling his family, but it seemed to be 'stay back, this is mine' or 'stay away, don't hurt him.'" This posturing hap-pened several times, Brian says, with Jambo blocking the other animals from approaching.

And then, "the boy woke up."

In a recording of the incident, taken from Brian's camera, you can hear the boy's mom screaming at him to stay still. But the boy was scared and hurt, and probably didn't realize where he was and that he was in danger. He began wiggling around and crying loudly, both things you shouldn't do with an unpredictable wild animal eyeing you. It was a terrifying moment for the people above (especially mom and dad), watching the apes, wondering if the situation would turn ugly. Would the animals attack?

They didn't. There was a collective sigh of relief from above. Meanwhile, zoo staffers were in the pen, working to round up Jambo and his family and get them inside. A paramedic leaped into the pit with a rope, and the team managed to lift the child out of the enclosure with help from above.

WESTERN LOWLAND GORILLAS

These gorillas, specifically Binti Jua's subspecies, *Gorilla gorilla gorilla*, are the most widespread and numerous of the gorillas in the wilds of Africa. In the last two decades, their populations have been shrinking because of poaching, habitat loss, and disease.

The boy's injuries weren't life threatening, fortunately, and the incident ended without anyone else getting hurt. Meanwhile, the story of what happened spread like wildfire, and Jambo was called a hero. Had he truly been protecting the child? It certainly seemed so. The massive beast could have turned against the boy, an intruder in his space. He could have let the other apes get their hands on him. He did neither. It may not have seemed so then, but it was one little boy's lucky day.

Though I reached out to Lamar, the boy (now an adult with a family of his own), to see what he recalled of his experience with the good-guy gorilla, I wasn't able to get his comments in time for publication. But no doubt he has opened his own child's eyes to the amazing kingdom of animals and the truth that sometimes, the biggest, scariest creature turns out to be the gentlest giant of all.

Parrot's Alarm

FIRST, A LITTLE ANIMAL ANATOMY LESSON. BIRDS DON'T have the stretchy mouth, larynx, and vocal chords that let us humans babble up a storm. Instead they have a special organ called a syrinx (like our larynx) that sits at the low end of the windpipe in the chest. When syrinx membranes quiver, they make sounds that rise up the throat and land in the mouth. That's when parrots, the talkers of the bird world, use their tongues to shape them into words. (Birds like vultures that don't have a syrinx can only hiss or grunt.)

Now, who isn't amused by the parrot who picks up a punch line, lets a little gossip slip, or reveals the favorite bad word of its owner?

But a bird named Willie took his talent to new heights, amazing listeners more than amusing them, when he blurted out the words that saved a little girl's life.

Meagan Howard was babysitting that day in 2006. She and close friend Samantha Kuusk, both students, were living together in Denver. On mornings when Samantha had class, Meagan would watch her two-year-old daughter, Hannah. Also part of the household was Meagan's pet, Willie, a parrot called a Quaker—a particularly intelligent and chatty breed that loves to clown around. Willie was indeed funny and a terrific talker. In addition to a few off-color words learned from Meagan's dad, he picked up quite a healthy vocabulary ("Silly Willie" was a favorite saying) and became a great mimic—of cats, dogs, chickens, and humans kissing. Plus, he could do a spot-on whistle of the *Andy Griffith Show* theme song.

With Samantha at school, Hannah had perched herself in front of morning cartoons while Meagan fussed in the kitchen, preparing the little girl her favorite breakfast treat, a Pop-Tart. When the toaster spit out the pastry, Meagan placed it at the center of the kitchen table to cool. She peeked at Hannah and, confident the child was fully engaged with the TV, slipped out quickly to use the bathroom.

QUAKER PARROT

Quaker parrots, also called monk parrots, can adapt easily to urban areas. In fact, pet monk parakeets who were set free by owners or escaped from shipping crates have settled into large feral flocks in many cities in the United States.

Meagan, Hannah, and a distracted Willie.

Willie at home.

"I was gone maybe thirty seconds," Meagan recalls. "And suddenly, I heard the bird." Willie was "going crazy, squawking and shrieking." She heard two very distinct words from the parrot's mouth. *Mama. Baby.* Repeated over and over again. "Mama! Baby! Mama! Baby!" Meagan ran out of the bathroom to find Hannah in the kitchen, holding the partly eaten Pop-Tart, gasping for air, her face and lips a terrifying shade of blue. And Willie still shrieking his refrain.

"Hannah had climbed up on a chair and gotten the Pop-Tart, and she was clearly choking on it," says Meagan. "I grabbed her and immediately started doing the Heimlich maneuver until the piece came flying out." The bird quieted down and Meagan burst into tears, relief washing over her: Hannah was fine, already smiling her big smile, not phased at all by the series of events that had her babysitter's heart drumming at top speed.

It was just a few minutes later that Samantha came home, walking in on her weeping friend and happy daughter—who was running around as if nothing were amiss. "Meagan had her head down when I came in. I kept asking her what was wrong," Sam recalls. "She finally said Hannah had given her a heart attack and told me the story."

"She was so grateful, thanking me for what I did," Meagan says, "but I said, don't thank me! It was Willie who was the hero!"

Samantha, after her shock and concern passed, was amazed. "I've heard stories of animals doing things like this, but this is a bird. It kind of blew my mind. He was always protective of children, but thank goodness he had the vocabulary to do what he did."

But what's really surprising, the women say, is that though Willie knew the word *mama*, he'd never before combined it with the word *baby*. And he hasn't said them together since. Without his noisy alert, Meagan says, "I would have had no idea what was going on. It could have been tragic. But he somehow knew something wasn't right; Hannah wasn't playing and talking like she usually does. He must have sensed she was in trouble and that someone needed to help her."

Samantha had always had a soft spot for her friend's pet, but after that, "the soft spot grew and grew. She was just so grateful," Meagan says. "I know Willie will forever be Sam's hero." (Samantha agrees.) Modestly, Meagan adds, "I did what anyone else would have done, but he did something really special."

The lucky dog.

The Seal Who Buoyed the Sinking Mutt

HOW CAN THIS BE: A STORY ABOUT A DOG AND A RES-cue in which the dog isn't the hero? Yes, indeed. It's atypical, but every once in a while even a canine gets in over its head and needs a little propping up.

Chris Hines and his son were walking their two dogs along the River Tees, in Middlesbrough, England, heading toward Newport Bridge. They were following a footpath that lay parallel to the water when Chris noticed a lone dog below them, at the base of the river wall. And something was very wrong with it. "I could see it was soaking wet and had been injured," he recalls. "It had a hole in its head! And it was really, really scared."

Chris handed his leashed dogs to his son, and told him to call for help in case the injured dog's owner was in trouble somewhere nearby. He then climbed down the wall to the river's edge and tried to coax the frightened animal toward him. But the panicked dog backed away, then leaped into the water and began frantically paddling away. And quickly, the river took control.

"There's a fast current at the center," Chris says. "The river flows into the North Sea not far from that spot, and the dog was being carried in that direction. It was being pulled under, too. It wasn't going to make it."

And then a smooth, gray head popped up like a puppet, not far from where the dog was struggling. "I thought it was a diver at first," Chris says, "but then I saw the big eyes and realized it was a seal. Seals often come into the river to go after the salmon, so I'd seen them around before. But this one did something totally unexpected."

As Chris watched, the seal swam to the drowning dog, dove beneath him, and lifted him upward. Soon, the dog was moving not toward the river's mouth but toward the far bank, pushed along by the animal beneath. "I couldn't believe what I was witnessing," says Chris. When the seal-propelled dog reached the edge, he tried to scramble onto the bank. It took a few tries, and a few pushes by the seal, before he gained a foothold. He sat there awhile, panting heavily, exhausted and, hopefully, humbled. The seal remained close, watching, bobbing on the water's surface, and then Chris noticed two other seals nearby, also with eyes on the dog. Finally,

A seal peeking above the surface, like this one, spotted the drowning dog.

the three gray heads disappeared under the water, one by one, as the seals slipped away. Says Chris, "The whole episode was absolutely brilliant to see!"

Now, by the time the dog had reached the far bank, Mark Baxter, then a firefighter from the Stockton Station, had arrived at the bridge with other rescuers. He, too, saw the dog emerge from the river, but from a vantage point closer to the action. And in

Common seals can stay underwater for nearly half an hour.

Mark's recollection, those other seals actually helped push the pup out of the water. "At first I thought they were attacking him, but that was far from the truth! They saved that mutt from the river, and it was clear they'd made a conscious decision to help. They're intelligent animals and I guess they sensed the dog's distress."

The near-death swim must have washed away all impulses to flee. The soggy dog sat still as Mark approached and got an arm around him. Others then wrapped the dog in blankets and took him to a clinic to get his head wound (cause unknown) treated.

Meanwhile, word quickly got out, as it always does, about the seal(s) that saved the dog, and news outlets were soon clamoring to report the story.

As the dog was tended, rescuers canvassed the area, still concerned that the dog's owner, now known to be an elderly man, might have fallen into the water. A lifeboat swept through, just in case. Fortunately, it turned out that the man had been napping at home during the entire ordeal. The dog had trotted off that morning, apparently seeking a solo adventure. Probably not the one he found.

HARBOR SEALS

Harbor seals, also known as common seals, can dive to 300 feet and stay submerged for nearly a half hour. They can even sleep underwater. A seal's nervous system has something akin to a shutoff switch that keeps the animal from breathing at the wrong time.

So what of the hero, or heroes, of this tale? The seals of Newport Bridge no doubt continued their comings and goings, but they never sought a photo op, never barked to claim credit for their good deed. And in truth, their actions don't make much sense according to the rules of nature. Why would wild marine creatures choose to assist a domestic land mammal who had nothing to give back? Was it just an instinctive response to an animal in distress?

Or maybe, just maybe, it was a simple act of kindness in a rough-and-tumble world. Let's go with that, shall we?

The Mare Who Stopped the Mad Cow

IN THE TOWN OF CASTLE DOUGLAS IN THE GALLOWAY Hills, in southwest Scotland, Fiona Boyd lives on a dairy farm with her husband and two sons. Fiona works at a school for special-needs children and volunteers with a group that offers horseback riding for the disabled. Horses have been part of her life since she started riding at age nine.

"From the first time I sat on a pony's back, I knew I was in love," she told me. "I love the way they smell, the way they nicker to say hello. And I love that when you blow softly into their noses, they blow softly back." As a child, she says, she would go for long walks with her animals, telling them about her day, and they would twitch their ears as if listening to her every word. "Even now, when they're just out in the field grazing or being silly—galloping about and kicking out—they make me happy," she says. "They make great friends."

Fiona's fondness for horses clearly runs deep. But there is one animal in particular who has a permanent home in her heart.

On a summer afternoon back in 2007, Fiona stepped outside into the warm, golden sunlight. One of the cows had recently given birth and Fiona needed to move mother and baby to the steading area, a building where calves are kept during their first days. There were six cows in the field, plus the calf, and Fiona, ignoring the adults, went straight to the young animal, prodding it to move toward the farm buildings.

And that's when trouble began. "The calf started bellowing for its mother," Fiona says, "which encouraged all the animals to come over and investigate."

Now, those of us who don't work with livestock might think of cows as passive beasts, standing still or at most moving in slow motion, chewing their cud and dropping cow pies here and there. They don't seem terribly interested in what's going on around them. And the random mooing doesn't exactly boost their air of authority.

But there's another side to cows, a very protective one. To defend her baby, a new mother can quickly

MAMA COWS

Cows form long-lasting friendships. They often have best friends, and will become distressed if separated from one another. Though they spend their lives with a herd, a few hours before giving birth, a mother cow will wander off alone to make a soft, grassy bed for calving, her special solo act.

turn fierce and dangerous. And that's the side of cow 62 (Fiona says they don't name the cows because they have so many) that emerged that summer afternoon. One minute Fiona was walking beside the calf, and the next she was being head-butted in the side by a very unhappy mother. The animal hit her hard, knocking her to the ground. "Before I could get up and run," Fiona recalls, "she began attacking me with her head and feet. I was terrified the other cows would join in—that's common with these animals." Fiona could see the farm's electric fence not far from where she lay, and she knew she had to get behind it to be safe.

But getting away wouldn't be easy. The angry cow stood directly over her, straddling her body, ready and able to crush the woman with its full weight. "I curled into a small ball, waiting for it to be over," Fiona says. The cow could kill her, she knew, but what could she do?

And then Fiona's savior burst onto the scene, turning potential tragedy into a true fairy tale. It was a beautiful chestnut Arab mare named Kerry, and when Fiona heard the animal neighing and snorting nearby, she felt a shiver of hope. "The next thing I know, there she is, and she's lashing out at the cow with her legs!" Fiona was amazed. The fifteen-year-old mare kept at it until the cow ran away, "then she stayed with me as I crawled a few yards to get behind that fence." Once Fiona was no longer in the danger zone between cow and calf, the horse calmed down and went back to munching on grass as if she hadn't just saved a human life.

Bleeding and hurting all over but grateful the episode was over, Fiona pried her phone from her jeans pocket and called her husband, who was working on another farm property about a mile and a half down the road.

He raced to where Fiona sat wounded on the ground, gathered her up, and rushed her to the hospital. Fortunately, no bones were broken. But she was bruised inside and out, and her back felt twisted and her spine out of place. It was a while before she could walk properly again.

"I should have been more aware of what I was doing," Fiona says now, "getting between mother and calf. The cow was only protecting her baby. I don't blame her at all." After the incident, though, whenever Fiona or her boys went into that field, Kerry would canter over and walk beside them like a bodyguard. "The cows were terrified of her," Fiona says. "I think she liked that."

As for Kerry's heroic actions, Fiona says she's always believed that if you love and treat your animals well, they will love and protect you in return. "I'd say Kerry proved me right."

A mother rescues her baby from a muddy pool.

One Elephant's Startling Compassion

IF I COULD CHOOSE A MOTHER FROM THE ANIMAL KING-dom to be my own, I'd pick an elephant. First, what parent could be more wonderfully strange than this plodding giant in a wrinkled gray suit—a mom who would nuzzle my neck with her cartoonish snout (one that contains some 100,000 muscles)? And no doubt she'd let me get as muddy as I pleased.

More important, there may be no beast more committed to her young, none more likely to act if I were stranded in the river or being stalked by a hungry lioness. From what I know of elephants, the adult females play the part of hero on a regular basis. The matriarch, who is top dog in an elephant herd, is leader, protector, and often savior.

Another mother defends her calf against hyenas.

Many stories celebrate mother elephants doing the heroic things that come naturally—taking care of family whatever the threat. In Botswana, one female raged against a pack of eighteen hyenas that attacked her calf. Witnesses say she shrieked and kicked up dust at the attackers, her ears flapping, until the hyenas took off running, hunched and humbled. Other than a lost tail, the calf was unharmed thanks to its mother's fierce defense.

And in a wildlife park in Cantabria, Spain, a mother elephant was filmed scooping her baby from the mouth of a muddy pool that threatened to suck the calf under. It was likely not the first time she'd had to sweep him out of danger. Speedy river rapids try to claim young animals, and mother elephants have been seen pushing them to shore. Sometimes other females rush over to join these rescues—especially if the mother is inexperienced and panicking—reaching their own trunks toward the little one, the elephant version of helping hands.

But however heroic they may be as parents, elephants,

particularly males, have a darker side. Where humans and elephants overlap, the animals do a lot of damage—tearing up crops and crashing through structures, destroying human livelihoods with stomping feet and a few swipes of a trunk. Elephants, of

This is believed to be the suddenly gentle elephant.

course, need land and food to survive. So do we. And where villages consume wilderness and block elephant migration routes, standoffs happen, and they rarely end well. Occasionally, people are injured or even killed.

So it was particularly perplexing, and comforting, to hear how a problem elephant's recent rampage through a home in India ended with a gentle gesture that actually saved the life of a child.

According to reports, one evening in Olgara Village, West Bengal, India, where people worship the Hindu elephant-headed god Ganesha, a lone forest elephant broke down a door and crashed through the wall of a house. (The same elephant had been blamed previously for other destructive stampedes and even deaths in the area.) The flimsy structure was no match for the huge animal, and pieces of the home rained down.

But then came a sound that changed everything. The elephant suddenly found himself standing over the bed of a crying child. And he stopped his devastating charge. For some reason, instead of ignoring the baby, swiping her aside, or escaping the crying sound by running away, the animal stretched out his trunk and began to pluck debris off the cot, cleaning up all the rubble that had fallen on and around the little girl.

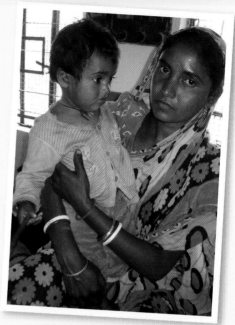

The lucky little girl.

Her parents, having heard the commotion, rushed in to help and were stunned to witness this suddenly thoughtful, even tender, effort from an animal that had seemed bent on destruction moments before. It was as if an empathy switch were flipped in the elephant's brain, perhaps by the sound of the girl's distress. (Elephants are known to respond to a herd-mate's sounds of suffering with caresses and soothing chirps and rumbles.) To the child's parents, it was simply a miracle. And then came a second miracle of sorts: The elephant turned and walked away, returning to the forest without further commotion.

Most likely the destroyer-turned-hero was a male that had come to scour the village in search of food, a not-uncommon scenario in rural areas at forest edges. Female elephants stick with the herd for life while males venture out on their own after puberty. So any solo animal is more likely to be a "he" than a "she."

BIG TALKERS

Elephants chat before going on a journey. A matriarch's deep, soft rumble spurs a "conversation" among the animals ahead of their departure. The animals' deepest sounds, at very low frequencies, travel as vibrations through the earth, allowing information to flow from afar.

Importantly, in giving this elephant credit for its good deed, I do not mean to minimize the destruction he caused, the terror that villagers feel facing off with these wild animals, nor the tragic outcomes of similar encounters. It's a sad reality that humans and elephants have become foes in some parts of the world simply because both are fighting to survive.

So when the worst can happen but doesn't, and when an animal shows compassion where none seemed possible before, it is a hopeful thing. There is no question that real damage was done (though fortunately the little girl's injuries from the falling debris weren't life threatening). But to at least one mother and father, the elephant that did harm is a hero nonetheless. How apt to this story that Hindus describe their elephant-headed deity as a destroyer of obstacles and a god of luck and of "opening the way."

The
maternal
tomcat.

The
Male Cat Mama

LET'S CONSIDER, FOR A MOMENT, THE MALE CAT. NOT the pudgy one sprawled on the sofa, legs akimbo, waiting for a belly rub. I'm talking about a scruffy feral feline, the bony wild cat in the alley, shrieking up a storm. This is the cat that has no interest in getting close to you, who spends his life more like the cats of old—outdoors, fending for himself.

Feral he-cats tend to have a "survival of the fittest" attitude. Life without a warm kitty bed and regular bowls of kibble can be tough, and cats gone wild aren't likely to seek or offer up affection.

And yet, this happened.

The whole thing started, says Sabrina Cantrell of the Central Oklahoma Humane Society, when the sky changed suddenly to the shade of a day-old bruise. The storm promised to be a rip-roaring, wind-spinning powerhouse. Many people had evacuated the area, while a few stayed behind at the animal shelter to prepare, readying crates and equipment to handle the deluge of creatures who would soon need help.

The storm arrived, and it was a monster, as predicted. It crushed homes and crumbled buildings. Black ink stained the sky, marking the tornado's path as it rolled across the land.

Sabrina is both a (people) nurse and a veterinary assistant, so she was prepared to handle whatever living things needed her most. That turned out to be the four-legged ones. She headed to the Humane Society's quarantine facility, where she and other staff would triage the wounded, trying to save as many as they could. "I knew we were in for a very long night," she says.

She was right. First came the horses. A huge farm had been hit head-on, and some injuries were so bad the animals had to be put down. Then word came that truckloads of injured dogs and cats would be delivered shortly. Initially it was mostly canines. Then came an onslaught of very wet, very unhappy cats.

"Animals like cats and dogs, when they sense a storm coming, usually try to take cover," Sabrina explains, "but that's not always a good thing. That cover might collapse or be blown away, and cats especially can be lifted by the wind and carried a long distance." The survivors end up with lacerations, broken bones, deep wounds from flying debris, "plus they're terrified and ready to bite our heads off if we try to help."

Still, help them the team did. Then Sabrina was asked to take one more roughed-up cat who had been found cowering in the debris of a fallen building. When the soft crate arrived, Sabrina unzipped it and looked in. Eyes as big as saucers were embedded in a creature so mud-caked it was hard to identify the species. "We first threw some warm towels in the bag, to make the wet, cold animal more comfortable," she recalls. "But we needed to give it fluids and to examine it more closely."

It wasn't easy to see beneath the muck. It took several volunteers to extract the terrified animal, hold it steady, and check it over. "We cleaned its eyes and ears—they were just clotted with mud—and patted it down in search of injury." It seemed to be impaled by something, but what? "There was something odd about the animal's shape, something

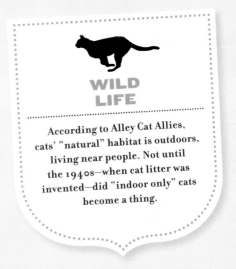

WILD LIFE

According to Alley Cat Allies, cats' "natural" habitat is outdoors, living near people. Not until the 1940s—when cat litter was invented—did "indoor only" cats become a thing.

wrong with its chest." Sabrina lifted up the cat's grimy arm to look, and suddenly, like a mini alien, "a little teeny head turned and looked at me! I was really confused until I saw that it was a kitten." Sabrina assumed then that she had a mother and baby on her hands.

"I didn't want to pull the kitten off, in case it was injured, so we continued cleaning them as one," Sabrina says. But once the baby began squirming around without obvious pain, it was time to separate the two for treatment. "I went to grab the baby, but the mom latched on harder, arms wrapped around the tiny thing, which couldn't have been more than a few weeks old." When she was finally able to pry mother from kitten, "the adult was clawing and batting us, trying to get the baby back."

The surprise came a little later. The baby was now washed and dried, amazingly unhurt in any way. When Sabrina went to check on the mother (also uninjured), the elder cat was standing up in the crate. And that's when Sabrina saw them. Testicles.

"An unneutered male! I couldn't believe it," she says. "This was no mama, and likely not even the papa." A feral male cat is a most unlikely kitten-sitter, she says. "I was so torn about reuniting them, because this was so unnatural. Why was this male taking care of this kitten? But I decided to chance it and put the two back together, just for a few minutes."

She did, and the animals immediately snuggled up together, no sign of confusion or aggression. Like a baby and its . . . mother.

However, to his human caregivers the male turned more ornery with time. Sabrina realized he would soon be impossible to handle, so she had to take the kitten away again while she still could. "We put it in its own crate with heating packs and a tiny teddy bear, and soon enough, the kitten was asleep in the bear's lap. When an animal can sleep, it means it feels secure, so it really brought tears to my eyes to see this."

The recovered male was eventually placed at a farm where cats live in a barn (with food and water) and roam free. And after a great deal of care, the kitten, too, found a home—with a loving woman who also took in a dog rescued after the storm. The animals, of course, became quick friends.

Sabrina still can't help but wonder at the strange behavior of the male cat. "Who would have thought that the protective arms of a feral male would be responsible for this itty-bitty baby's life? He might have killed it. But instead, he heroically saved it. It's a beautiful thing."

Safe from the storm, the kitten falls asleep.

Without Yoda (above) and Coco (right) their owner might not have escaped her burning house.

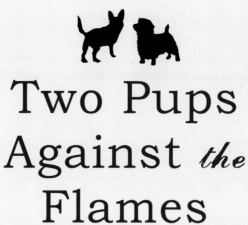

Two Pups Against *the* Flames

IT WAS ALREADY A WRETCHED DAY FOR **CHRISTY BOGNER.** She'd gotten a call in the afternoon that her grandma had died, and through the evening hours, she'd wept uncontrollably. It was the kind of crying that drains you until you're an empty shell. The only good thing about it is, afterward, you collapse into a bottomless sleep. That's just what Christy did.

Except for her two dogs and a barn cat that sometimes found its way into the house, Christy was alone that Sunday night. In one bit of good fortune, both of her young daughters were at sleepover parties. At bedtime, Coco, Christy's Yorkshire terrier, was curled up on her pillow. And her tiny mutt, Yoda—named for his stick-up-straight ears that reminded the family of the *Star*

Wars character—was tucked under the blankets at her feet, where he always slept. The bedroom door was closed.

At about 4 a.m., Coco started barking. She licked her owner's face and Christy, barely awake and assuming the dog wanted to go outside, pleaded for another few hours of sleep. She began to drift back off, but the barking continued. Coco then began pawing at the blankets, trying to free Yoda from his bedding wrap.

"Finally, I woke up enough to figure out what was happening," Christy says. "I saw a haze of smoke, so I jumped up and opened the door. The fire was already halfway up the stairs." The nineteenth-century farmhouse (which Christy had spent five years renovating) had a main staircase in front and vintage "servants" stairs in back. She realized the back way was the only way out. Coco continued barking and pacing by the door that was licked by flames. "I grabbed Yoda off the bed. He was really scared and was wiggling around. I called for Coco to follow as I staggered toward the back. But Coco didn't follow."

COCO & YODA

These two brave pups both received the Kansas Veterinary Medical Association 2013 Hero Pet of the Year award.

Christy chokes up as she tells this part of the story (and I suspect readers will, too). "Coco didn't follow," she repeats. "Instead she ran right toward the flames, barking at them. I tried to grab her but couldn't. She kept going as if she could fight the fire herself." Coco's cries still ring in Christy's ears.

That's when Christy, overcome by smoke, ran out of breath and fell down the back stairs. As she collapsed, Yoda leaped from Christy's arms and ran back into the bedroom to find his friend. "I doubt he got very far," Christy says. "His little lungs just couldn't take it." He, too, succumbed to the fire.

Christy, meanwhile, managed to fumble her way to the back door and outside. "By the time I got out, flames had consumed my bedroom, and the front half of the house was collapsing." She lived in a rural area with just one elderly couple nearby. Christy had left her keys in her car, a lucky thing, so she drove to their house—but no one answered there. "I had to drive into town to get help. It was a good thirty minutes. By the time I got back, the house was gone."

Christy spent several days in the hospital recovering from burns to her lungs and throat. But she was alive. And if it hadn't been for Coco, she has no doubt she would have died. "There's absolutely no way I would have made it out if Coco hadn't woken me. I had been so deeply asleep, so exhausted. Her persistence is what got me out of bed. And saved my life."

The recovery has been extremely painful for Christy—more mentally than physically. The loss of the dogs is one of the hardest things. She remembers how special the two of them were. "We got Coco for my daughter's eighth birthday. We actually met the breeder at a pizza place and right there made arrangements to get the last puppy in the litter!" And Yoda came from a close friend whose dog had had pups, so he was immediately a special part of the family.

Coco:
"the protective
one."

Yoda's ears reminded the family
of the Star Wars character.

Coco was the protective one, checking out new visitors thoroughly and keeping an eye on Christy's daughters (and alerting her with three barks if they were sneaking downstairs after bedtime!). Coco also mothered Yoda "like crazy," she says. "They were so funny and they really fed off each other, running and playing on the farm." Coco would chase fuzzballs in the air: "Suddenly she'd be jumping up and biting at nothing!" And Yoda loved to waltz, getting up on his hind legs if anyone said the word 'dance.' The dogs are very much missed, Christy says.

The cause of the fire remains a frustrating mystery. But Christy and the girls are now getting their lives back on track. Happily, that includes two new additions to the family. The friend's dog who gave birth to Yoda had another litter, so Christy and the kids grabbed up two pups. "Oprah and Gizmo!" Christy says. "And what's amazing is they are so much like Coco and Yoda were. Oprah looks much like Coco and is very affectionate, wanting to be with you all the time. Gizmo, who has Yoda ears, sleeps under the covers at my feet, just like Yoda did. It's weird, almost uncanny, how similar they are."

They're not replacements, of course. "These little guys are now here to help us move on," says Christy. But the family will never forget the original pair, funny little Yoda and valiant Coco with her lifesaving bark, her absolute refusal to back down when a fire tried to claim those she loved.

The Gentle Elk's Good Deed

THIS STORY IS ABOUT HOW AN ABSURDLY IMPROBABLE pair of animals got to know each other. Intimately.

Here's what happened. It was at the Pocatello Zoo in Idaho. There's a big pasture there, about 5 acres, where a host of animals intermingle peacefully, including bison, elk, antelope, and wild geese. Marmots live there, too—they're basically a big breed of squirrel—who are more than happy to help themselves to daily meals and are content to be among animals that don't prey on them. They do have to dodge stomping hooves as they scamper around, but generally they are safe from harm.

Except for this: Marmots, like other mammals, need air to breathe. Which they cannot do underwater. And occasionally one falls into a water trough when leaning in for a drink. If the water is low, the marmot may not be able to climb up the side of the trough to get back out. That makes for a bad day for the fallen marmot. Its last day, in fact.

But one marmot who inadvertently went swimming got thrown a very strange life preserver.

Joy Fox, a retired veterinarian, was a volunteer at Pocatello Zoo for four years. One day during her stint there, she and a zoo staff member were in the education building, which has big windows facing the pasture. Suddenly they noticed the elk named Shooter, the only male (bull) at the zoo at the time, acting very oddly. "He was pacing back and forth near the water trough, then he'd go to it and put his foot in there, pawing at the water," she recalls. "We had no idea what was going on, but it was pretty funny to watch. It was a hot day, so we thought maybe he was just playing, splashing around. I grabbed my camera and got some photos."

And then came the strangest part. "He kept repositioning himself, trying to get his face into the tank without his antlers bumping on the edges and holding him back. And suddenly, he jerked his head up and we could see something was in his mouth. It was a marmot!" He'd actually grabbed it by its head, she says, but surprisingly gently, using more lips than teeth.

Shooter lifts the drowning marmot from the trough.

As the two women watched, having gone outside and sneaked a little closer, Shooter let the animal plop to the ground, then stood over it, watching, sniffing, and gently pushing it with his hoof, perhaps seeking signs of life. The marmot, looking every bit the drowned rat, lay still for a moment, stunned from its ordeal. But then it woke up with a start and, realizing it was out in the open with a giant looming above, scooted under the water trough. It recovered there for a little while before taking off across the field, perhaps a bit humbled from its unintended swim and its intimate moment with an elk's lips.

Whether the elk just wanted *that thing* out of his water tank so he could drink unimpeded, or actually realized it was an animal in trouble, no one knows. Shooter was about four years old at the time (young for an elk), and though some zoo staff feared him for his size and dangerous antlers, he'd always been "a bit of a goof" in the pasture, Joy says, "always playing around with something or coming up to the fence for attention." Yet his actions at the tank were serious. He didn't turn the marmot into a toy, didn't bat it around once it was on the ground. He was curious, but gentle. "I think he sensed the animal was in distress. It was clear that he purposefully got it out of the water," she says. "He could have stomped on it or bitten down hard, but he didn't. Clearly he had no interest in hurting it."

"The time it took him to reposition himself, to get his head in there and make it happen—we could hardly believe what we'd seen," she says.

Zoo staffers have since placed concrete blocks in the bottom of the water tanks to give future fallen marmots a platform for escape. But Joy will always remember watching the big elk tilting his horned head this way and that, trying to get a grip on that little drowning animal before it was too late. "It was exciting and funny, such a unique moment, and I'm so glad we got to see it," she says.

I'm glad, too. Because if someone hadn't witnessed the scene, who would ever think to ascribe empathy to an elk?

ELK APPEAL

During mating season (also called the rut), bull elk will wallow in the mud, a behavior that, for some reason, makes the males more impressive, attractive, and better smelling to females.

The Bravest Little Llama

BRUCE SCHUMACHER KNOWS WHAT LOSS FEELS LIKE. Two years ago, as the man sat in a dentist's chair a few miles away, his home, vehicles, and barn—holding his past, present, and the future he'd envisioned—burned to the ground. An arsonist's flame sparked on a nearby highway had swept onto his 10 acres of land, and by the time he was notified of the tragedy and able to reach the scene, the fire had taken all Bruce had. (In total, some 1,200 acres were destroyed by the arsonist's terrible act.)

Bruce had lived on his southern California property, near the top of Cajon Pass in a town called Hesperia, for thirty-two years. The sixty-eight-year-old worked long hours as a psychiatric technician in a home for the criminally insane, and, more to his liking,

Bruce with Little Man.

cared for his many farm animals. His life-long fondness for all creatures had Bruce regularly rescuing the unwanted, including a sheep that had been mauled by wild dogs and a rooster with a peg leg. So though losing his home and much of what he owned was devastating, the death of many of his animals was the hardest to take.

In the end, the tally of victims was tragic. The fire took goats, alpacas, chickens, pigeons, geese, rabbits, dogs, a young ewe, and a donkey and her yearling. But where you find a fire, you are also likely to find a hero—maybe a neighbor who yells out that there's a baby in the house, or a firefighter who saves the family pet from a roomful of flames. In this case, the hero walked on four legs instead of two, and his actions saved not just one, but thirty living creatures.

Little Man was a whitish-coated llama with warm brown eyes. He'd previously belonged to a petite woman named Nancy, a long-time friend of Bruce's, but he'd gotten a little aggressive around her, as adult male llamas sometimes do. "For her safety, and because she knew I was interested in llamas, she offered him to me," Bruce says. The animal wasn't easy to convince: "He really wanted to stay with Nancy. She had raised and loved him." But eventually, Little Man became part of Bruce's menagerie. (As an aside, the llama had a thing for blondes, it appeared. Whenever Nancy would visit, Bruce said, "he'd cry his llama cry and try to lick her head. He always loved her curly blond hair!")

Little Man guided this flock to safety.

As Little Man got older, he proved himself a great friend to Bruce and a great protector to Bruce's sheep. Before the llama arrived, says Bruce, "the flocks were vulnerable. I had lost thirty-eight sheep in one year to coyotes. There was also a mountain lion around, and bobcats." Under Little Man's watch, "I didn't lose a single sheep to wild predators," Bruce marvels.

Bruce says whenever one of his ewes was giving birth, the others would form a circle around her, facing outward, to shield the new mother and her baby from any possible predators. "I saw Little Man doing that, too, standing over the mother to protect

LOADED-UP LLAMAS

Llamas make sturdy pack animals, but they do have limits. While a llama might cover 20 miles with 75 pounds on its back without complaint, an overloaded animal might lie down, spit, hiss, and kick until someone reduces the weight.

her. And he would lie still while baby sheep walked all over him and playfully pulled at his wool. He was like another parent to them." And when a predator was near, "Little Man would go over to the fence and make a threatening clicking noise, walking up and back, pacing until the threat had moved on."

On the day of the tragedy, Bruce was at the dentist when he heard that there was a fire in his part of town. He tried to go home, but to keep residents and pedestrians out of danger, firefighters had blocked the way into his neighborhood. He knew his ranch was in trouble. There was nothing he could do.

By the time Bruce was allowed back on his property, he found ashes where his house and barn had been—but also, something wonderful. Miraculously, around thirty sheep stood upright and unharmed. The whole flock, minus one young animal who had run off, was still alive. And there with them was their protector, Little Man.

"He was lying on the ground, as llamas do. He was alive, but his eyes were burned shut and his wool singed," Bruce says. Little Man's coat, in fact, had actually insulated him and kept the injuries from being worse. The flock was tucked in behind him, away from where the fire had been. "He'd clearly taken them to an area he felt was safe. And because of that, they all survived."

Little Man himself was in rough shape. Bruce could only assume that the llama put his body between the sheep and the flames as he herded them to safety. Bruce says when he saw the animal, "I just bent down over him and cried. I knew in my heart what he'd done for the others. I just said, 'oh, Little Man, you're okay . . .' but I knew he was in pain." The vet felt the llama might recover, and the local Llama Rescue Club sent members to offer what care they could.

But sadly, no efforts were enough to save the llama. The smoke he'd inhaled had injured his lungs, and a week later Little Man passed away.

The disaster hit Bruce very hard, and he is still struggling to get back on his feet. Some of his animals besides the sheep did recover, and he's grateful to have them around. But his sadness over the unlucky ones remains a weight on his heart. Of course, his most potent memory is of Little Man, who put aside any pain and fear of his own to protect those in his care. "I know llamas are devoted, but in such a crisis, would another animal stay put like he did?" Bruce asks. "Once he was injured, why didn't he simply try to save himself?"

"Because he was special," Bruce answers his own question. "He performed a miracle out of true devotion. He gave his life for those sheep. That's a real hero."

Cow 569 made a
moooody life preserver.

The Buoyant Bovine

SOME CALL IT THE SUMMER THAT NEVER WAS. AT LEAST they do in New Zealand. It was February 2004, normally warm and dry on North Island. But that year, torrential rains, and winds blowing as swiftly as a cheetah runs, turned open land into vast, muddy lakes. A 113-mile river called the Manawatu, which snakes through south central North Island, rose around 50 feet to its highest level since 1902. Hundreds of people moved to higher ground. But some rode out the disaster where they were.

"Crikey!" says dairy farmer Kim Riley, one who truly felt the full force of the storms. "It was some flood!"

At the time, Kim and her family worked a large dairy farm on a floodplain near the Manawatu, about 740 acres stocked with enough cows that, if you could stack them on end nose to tail, they'd bump into cruising jetliners.

When you have that many cows, Kim told me, giving them real names is more of an effort than it's worth. So they go by numbers, nice and simple, clearly visible on tags attached to their ears. This story is about cow 569, a stubborn and not particularly friendly girl, who ended up as a hero only begrudgingly. Still, a hero she was.

Dairy farmers rise before the sun, and on the morning of the incident, Kim was up by 4 o'clock to begin the day's milking. It's a big undertaking to get all the cows from the pasture to the dairy and get them milked, cleaned up, and out to new pasture. All 900 cows are milked twice a day, so the whole process is repeated in the afternoon.

The previous night had been one of heavy downpours, but still Kim was surprised by what she saw. "I could see the cows standing knee-deep in water. I needed to move the animals, but they got spooked in the dark and started to run," she says. "I tried to head them off, but suddenly, shockingly, there was no solid ground under my feet!" Kim and some 300 cattle were floating along together in warm, smelly, muddy water. It might sound to most of us like a reasonable time to panic, but Kim remained very calm. Rather than consider the danger, she thought, Oh goodness, I'll be late for milking!

Kim tried to swim, but her boots, leggings, and coat filled

Kim, with her hero.

with water, keeping her from moving far. As she struggled to yank off the gear, she could hear distressed cows calling out, looking for one other. In their haste to get their feet on the ground, "cows were swimming right over top of me. They have a strong dog paddle. I was just something in their way, an obstacle to get over, and they ignored me."

Pushed around and bruised, Kim continued to work against the flow. She knew the water was deep—her feet bumped the barbed wire that's stapled to the tops of the farm's fencing. Fortunately, "it wasn't a really strong current. The floodwaters were just eddying around." Still, she couldn't seem to get anywhere. She was stuck. And having been at it for 40 minutes, she was getting weary.

There's even a children's book about cow 569.

That's when she spotted cow 569. "She had peeled off from some other cows and was paddling hard, huffing as she swam. She was heading right at me!" Kim realized this might be her ticket ashore, so as the animal crossed in front of her, "I lunged for her neck and held on tight. I thought, if you're getting out of here, I'm going with you!"

The heat coming off the animal, its wet, grassy smell, and its pounding heart comforted Kim as she rode with the cow toward a hillside poking up above the water. "It happened in slow motion, very gracefully," she recalls. "I tried to make it easy for her, to stay streamlined lying against her side. Still, I don't think she was thrilled to have the extra weight. She was really huffing, like a horse after a heavy run."

When the pair reached the hill, Kim slid off the cow and tried to give her a good petting of thanks. But cow 569 wasn't much for affection, and she shrugged her owner off and moved out of reach. "She was probably just annoyed with me, more than anything," Kim says. "She was truly a no-fuss, no-nonsense animal, a very strong worker, bossy, always first to do everything, but not much of a love." Regardless, the cow was a hero, if an unintended one. Without the cow's strength and confident swim, and her tolerance of having a passenger, Kim might have drowned. Also, it turns out, cow 569 was pregnant during the ordeal, which somehow adds another layer to her accomplishment.

COW 569

Cow 569 was such an inspiring hero that her owner honored her in two books for kids: *Cow Power* and *Baby Cow Power*. The second book is about 569's calf, which was in utero during the lifesaving swim and was born six months later.

Not surprisingly, the heroic animal wasn't much for media attention, but she got plenty of it after saving Kim's life. She wasn't a looker, her owner recalls, with her funny face and bent ear, but the media snapped photos and gobbled up her story. The cow also endured the appreciation of her owners. "We'd give her a special little pat and say, 'Hello, you ugly old thing!' I think she knew we saw her as special, but she didn't seem to care."

Kim wrote two kids' books about cow 569 and her calf—born six months after the flood and unfazed by his in utero experience. "Cow 569 carried on working as a milking cow for years after that, until we retired her at age fourteen," Kim says. The animal's fan mail took some keeping up with, and the two made trips to schools, galas, and other events. The cow remained cranky, but was beloved nonetheless. Says Kim, "I'm grateful to 569, that ugly old thing!"

*Ramsey, safely back
on dry land.*

The Dog-Saving Dolphins

EVER SINCE I FIRST DIPPED A TOE IN THE SEA, I WAS sure that someday I would be "chosen" to bond with a wild dolphin. But other than some playtime with a relatively tame animal, it hasn't happened yet. Not to me, anyway.

There's an Australian woman named Karyn Gitsham, however, who has had many magical moments with heroic animals. She was saved from drowning by one of her dogs, a huge ridgeback named Winston. He sensed her peril and grabbed her by the back of her shirt, as if she were one of his pups, and pulled her from cold, deep water. And she was nearly crushed by a rearing stallion (she had fallen off and was lying beneath him), but she and the horse met eyes and he suddenly twisted his body, shifting

*Four dolphins, like this small group, came to
Ramsey and Karyn's rescue.*

his weight awkwardly and maybe painfully to avoid her. The horse fell on his back, leaving Karyn unscathed. When he finally roused himself, he came straight to her and put his head on her chest.

My favorite example of all: Karyn was sitting alone on a hill near her horse paddock, crying over the loss of her mother. She was rocking and weeping with her face in her hands. And then she looked up and saw that her horses, eight mares, had joined her on the hill, and were lying in a perfect circle around her. "It was like being encased in warmth and love," she says. "I could feel this calmness coming from them—they created a safe place for me to grieve."

Animals have saved Karyn in many ways, over and over again.

So I guess I shouldn't be surprised that Karyn got to have that dolphin experience that I always wanted. Here's her story.

Karyn lives on top of a hill on 7 beautiful acres that overlook the ocean, near Adelaide in South Australia. For years, each morning, she would take a long walk on the beach with her two dogs, Ramsey, a cocker spaniel, and Buddy, a Rhodesian ridgeback. Ramsey loves to swim and is pretty fearless for a little guy. So on this day back in 2008, he leaped into the surf and started paddling his furry little feet—and didn't stop. He swam and swam until he was just a tiny speck in the water, hard to spot with the sun glinting off the sea. Karyn kept calling him to come back, but he was determined, it seemed, to reach South Africa.

Not only was she worried that he could tire and drown, but "this is Jaws country," Karyn says. "We've got lots of great whites. I was horrified for him!" She moved down the beach, keeping him in sight, until she ran out of beach. "Now it was all rocks and a cliff face. But I thought, *I'm not going to lose my dog!* So I started scrambling. The water was crashing against the rocks—my adrenaline was pumping like mad." Buddy, meanwhile, was running along on an upper cliff, barking at his family down below. And Ramsey, it seemed, was now trying to swim to his owner—but he couldn't make any headway. He might have been caught in a riptide, a very dangerous situation.

And then things got worse. "I fell in," Karyn says.

Ramsey still swims, but is more cautious now, Karyn says.

Coughing and sputtering, she managed to grab on to a rock and hang on, but waves were crashing over her, and she was getting tossed around, sucked under, and beaten bloody. With Buddy helpless on shore, "I hung on for at least half an hour, calling to Ramsey. A few times, I let go to try to swim after him, but I was pushed back into the rocks. And soon, I couldn't see him anymore, and I thought, this is it. Ramsey is gone and I'm not going to make it. There's no one here to help me. This is the end."

I'm guessing, dear reader, that you know what's coming. A flipper knifed through the waves. Then another. And another! Plus a fourth, a tiny one. Four dolphins, one just a calf, came zipping in toward Karyn, then turned and swam out to where Ramsey had been. They disappeared underwater for a moment. And then, she saw him, his little head above water coming toward her. He appeared to be floating along without effort. The dolphins were pushing him! "When he got pretty close, I let go and started swimming hard to reach him," Karyn says. "I grabbed Ramsey and then felt nudges against my legs as the animals pushed me toward a big boulder. I managed to throw Ramsey on top and scramble up myself." Waterlogged, Ramsey and Karyn lay there panting, exhausted and stunned. "I saw the dolphins one more time," she says, "continuing on their way out to sea. I thought, what just happened?"

Karyn had dislocated her arm, torn a bicep muscle, and was scratched and bloodied from being thrown against the rocks. But she was alive and, miraculously, her little dog was, too.

Once the media frenzy died down, Karyn went back to her regular routine, walking the beach each morning. Buddy has since passed away, but Ramsey still goes along and still loves to swim. "But he doesn't go far and he always comes right back," she says. Now when she sees dolphins off-shore, which is nearly every day, Karyn feels a very special connection with them, an almost spiritual one. "Often I think it's the same pod that rescued us, so I put my hand out to them and close my eyes and think, *Thank you. Thank you.*" But she suspects they don't need any recognition for their heroic act. "It's just what they do, how they are," she says. "It's as we all should be."

DOLPHIN PODS

Common dolphins regularly gather in big social pods averaging hundreds of individuals. And occasionally, they create vast groups with upward of 10,000 animals, all moving together through the sea. This ocean spectacle is called a "mega pod."

Everyday Heroes

Living Lives of Giving

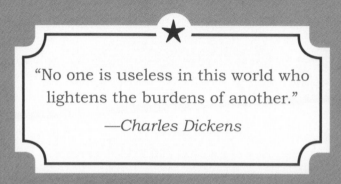

"No one is useless in this world who lightens the burdens of another."

—*Charles Dickens*

HERE ARE THE ANIMALS WHO AREN'T ONE-HIT WONDERS BUT generous all of their days. It takes a certain kind of temperament to do what they do, and not all have it. They remind us of what it means to offer oneself to others, fully and with a big heart.

The
Giving
Greyhound

THE DOG IN THIS STORY MIGHT JUST BE THE MOST GENEROUS- of-heart canine I've ever known. A hero in benevolence.

Now, grab a tissue. Here is the sad part. Dogs are abandoned every day around the world, left to fend for themselves. Some turn feral, tapping into dormant wild instincts for the tools to survive. Others simply give up, unable to muster the energy to live on. Young Jasmine, perhaps three years old, was one of the latter types—left in a cold groundskeeper's shed without food or water for an unknown number of days. As a greyhound, she would not have survived long—she had no thick warm coat, no fat to nourish her in lean times.

Fortunately, a policeman rescued the frightened pup after someone called the station about a barking dog. He soon brought her to Geoff Grewcock at the Nuneaton & Warwickshire Wildlife Sanctuary in England.

"She was lethargic. Matted up, full of fleas, covered in bald spots," Geoff recalls. "Her ears were all mucked up. She was in very bad shape." When he would approach her, "she would put her head down, cowering. She'd had a tough time."

It took a few months to rid her of her fears (and her fleas!), but finally something clicked in her. Despite the long face (she was a greyhound, after all), Jasmine's timidity and sadness passed. "It's as though she suddenly realized she'd been rescued, that she no longer had to be scared, and that it was time to give back," Geoff says.

That giving back became Jasmine's purpose. From then on, she put all of her energy into making other animals feel welcome, comfortable, and safe, just as Geoff and others at the sanctuary had done for her.

"At first, we just thought it was curiosity. Every time a new animal came into the sanctuary, she'd go and have a look." But there was something deeper happening in Jasmine. She really cared and wanted to help. "First thing in the morning, she'd go around to each cage and make sure everyone was all right," her owner says. She'd play with the birds—letting spring chicks sit on her nose and back, "wagging her tail in delight!" She'd stroll with the foxes like old friends (hounds are supposed to *chase* foxes), and dote on a badger whose life she'd helped save. If an animal was injured or frightened—including a rabbit that had a bald patch where someone had repeatedly kicked her—she'd sit with it nestled beside her, licking and nuzzling as she saw fit. She seemed to sense who was abused, who was hurt, who just needed a little mothering or a playmate, and adjusted accordingly. "It didn't matter what it was. Sometimes at night, it was hard to get her out of the other animals' pens."

In fact, remember Bramble, the little deer featured in *Unlikely Loves* with his turkey pal, Tinsel? In that book, I mentioned that a dog first roused the deer from his coma. That was Jasmine. Her soft licks brought the animal around and she then posted herself by his side, keeping the little guy's spirits up and helping him heal. "She's a big part of the reason Bramble survived," Geoff says.

Then there's this. Ready the tissues again, folks: One day, two 8-week-old terrier pups were brought into the sanctuary. They had been tied to the railroad tracks and left to die. Thankfully, someone rescued them before a train rumbled in, but of course they were terribly stressed by their ordeal. When they were dropped off, they refused to move or be moved. Before Geoff could even try to handle them, Jasmine stepped in. "She

AWARDS & HONORS

Jasmine won the Shining World Loving-Care Award on behalf of Supreme Master Ching Hai in 2009.

immediately went over, picked up the first one by the scruff of the neck, crossed through the sanctuary into the house, dropped it on the [couch], then went back for the other one," he recalls. The dog then settled herself between the two and stayed there all day. She became their constant companion for about two weeks, until they felt safe enough to interact with others and explore on their own. "She knew something was wrong and wanted to care for them," Geoff says. "It was fantastic."

In fact, there was no animal that Jasmine didn't welcome and embrace at the sanctuary. Geoff guesses she doted on at least fifty different creatures of many species during her time there. And when she passed away in 2011 at age fourteen, "all the animals went very quiet," he says. "My other dogs seemed forlorn. It took a couple of weeks before they acted normal again." He and his family were crushed by the loss, too, "but with one hundred fifty other animals to care for, we had something to focus on every day," he says.

She was a mother and guardian, a real hero, to so many, Geoff marvels. She was even a teacher: One of the dogs she adored seems to have learned from her kindness and is now playing a Jasmine-like role at the sanctuary. "Certain animals aren't just passing through. . . . They're here doing something special," says Geoff. "That was Jasmine."

Getting a nuzzle from Bramble the deer.

The Compassionate Camel

SERGEANT BERT HAS A HUGE HOLE IN HIS UNIFORM, BUT he's never been reprimanded for it. The gap is just part of his unique look around the sheriff's office. I'll say this, though: Good thing he's a dromedary instead of a Bactrian or he'd have barely any uniform at all.

Bert, of course, is a camel. (Dromedaries have one hump, Bactrians have two.) He's of the one-humped variety (thus the single hole in his clothes), a big-muzzled giant—now 2,100 pounds—born and raised in California. And he's done good things for a long list of people. He's been so active in the community, in fact, that the Los Angeles County Sheriff's Department in San Dimas gave him a badge and a title. (No gun, though.)

Bert on a reenactment trek.

Bert, who was a deputy before being promoted to sergeant, has made great use of his status. He's regularly at schools helping convince kids to stay away from drugs. He visits hospitals, where he brings out the happy in sad people. He's in parades and goes to parties. He sticks his big nose into kids' Halloween bags and steals their candy, and grabs hats off of heads and holds them just out of reach, to everyone's delight. He spends time with blind kids letting them dig their hands into his furry neck. He stars in his own Bert coloring books and baseball cards. His owner, Nance Fite, herself an LA County Sheriff's Department reserve deputy, says, "Everybody loves Bert."

Nance says there are endless stories to share about Bert championing people in need, but she has a favorite. "I took him to a children's hospital and the nurse wheeled out a little boy to meet him," she recalls. "This boy was very ill and hadn't smiled or even moved much in about six months. I brought Bert over to him and the animal must have sensed the boy's need; he put his head right in the kid's lap and stayed that way, motionless."

As the nurses, parents, and Nance watched, there was a transformation. "I could tell the boy with every fiber of his being was trying to lift his hand to pet Bert," Nance says. "And then he started giggling! We were all crying. It was unbelievable to see the boy feeling happy after so long. I think that moment is why Bert was put on this earth."

Now, I know what you're thinking. Camels are mean. They stink. They spit (or, more accurately, they projectile vomit—nice, huh?). They're total curmudgeons in the world of hoofed mammals. It's okay to say it. Camels do not make good pets. Right?

The pet thing is for the most part true, so please do not try this at home. But is it true that all camels are curmudgeons? Nance thinks not. "I think camels are born as gentle creatures, with brains and fortitude," she says. "A few stay mostly gentle and jovial, but others feel they have to defend themselves on various levels. Camels don't put up with things they deem as bad." Thus, the bad rap.

Bert is certainly exceptional. A reputation-busting camel. A sweet camel with amazing instincts about people.

Perhaps among the explanations for his kind heart are the unlikely loves he's had in his life. At five months old, when Bert was already in Nance's care, her elderly horse and her dog both decided the camel was the family baby. They provided him with a lot of affection. And when he grew to be a giant among them, he realized he had to be gentle or risk hurting those who were good to him. "I think that's why he is so good with children now," says Nance. "He lets them crawl all over him. He's very careful with small things." (One duck underfoot was sacrificed for this lesson, but the camel never repeated that mistake!)

Not only has Bert been good to kids, but he's been Nance's hero as well. Some years ago, Nance and a group of others were camping out. They'd been reenacting a historic camel trek. "I was in my tent and Bert was in a corral nearby, but he kept bawling and screaming, fretting and pacing," Nance recalls. "I kept going over there to calm him but he wouldn't stop." So Nance moved her tent closer to Bert, thinking maybe that would soothe him. "He lay down with his nose inside my tent and slept there all night," she says. And the next morning, "We woke to find huge mountain lion tracks all around the area. He must have known it was there and was only happy when he was close enough to me to protect me."

Bert inspires countless kids on his school visits.

He has even helped her to be a better person, she says. "I've become more tolerant of a lot of things," she says. "I've learned to be more patient. You can't force a 2,100-pound camel to do something he doesn't want to do. It has to be his idea or it won't happen. That's been a good lesson for me."

But it's his work with young people that truly makes this dromedary unique, Nance says. "After our school sessions, kids will yell promises to Bert that they'll stay safe and off drugs. Teachers rave about how effective his visits are. We go to see at-risk youths, and do programs in rough neighborhoods. He's such an icebreaker. Everyone around him just has to giggle when he puts his head down and smooches on a kid or makes his low, guttural sounds." As we all know, it isn't easy to get kids to listen to good advice. But Bert has a knack for it. "Instead of shoving a BE GOOD message down kids' throats," Nance says, "he gets them excited about doing the right thing." Just his presence seems to do wonders, she says.

"I love sharing this special animal with others," says Nance. "And he just loves getting out there and doing his thing."

The Dog Who Loved Cats

OFTEN, IT GOES LIKE THIS: CAT SPOTS DOG, HUNKERS down, freezes. Dog, goofy and distracted, might not see cat at first. But then, a tail twitch draws its eye. Cat! Dog moves in. Cat's eyes go wide as it growls that low growl. Dog wags tail and drops to its haunches, cornering cat. Cat hisses, spits, and bats at canine muzzle, waits a beat, then slips away. Cat was right all along. Stupid, irritating dog not worthy of attention.

But Wuffy would prove that mad cat wrong. Wuffy, a mutt with a shar-pei for a father and a mystery mother, did more than get along with cats. She saved them. Hundreds of them. She nursed sick cats back to health, and she eased abandoned kittens' fears and got them eating. She knew what a hurt cat needed and she provided it. It was instinctive, and she was passionate about what she did, giving most of her long life to this job.

When all this began, Wuffy's owner, Gary Rohde, was not what you'd call a "cat person." In fact, he really didn't like cats at all.

But Gary adored Wuffy, so he had to make peace with his least-favorite creatures. "This cat thing, it's what Wuff was born to do, so I had no choice but to accept them," he says.

It all started one summer day back in 1995, when Gary saw Wuff rummaging around in the backyard bushes. "She came out with a little kitten in her mouth. She was holding it by the scruff, just like a mama cat would do." Gary told Wuff to "release" and she dropped her prize into his hands. Then she dove back into the bushes. "She brought out number two, then three. She was like Houdini! Finally, out came a fourth. No mother cat in sight."

Wuffy mothering two kittens.

Gary put the mewing newborns into a box and took them to his vet, hoping the doctor could find them homes.

"But Wuffy went stark raving mad," he says. "She was chewing at the box,

Gary guesses that Wuffy "rescued" 500 to 700 cats and kittens.

pawing it, didn't want to leave it. She wanted her kittens!"

The kittens were just about two weeks old and would need special care and milk every couple of hours. The vet suggested Gary take them to a local animal shelter, where there might be a nursing mother cat able to take them on. But there wasn't one. So someone would have to start, right away, feeding them with a bottle and taking care of their every need, getting them beyond their newborn stage so they'd be strong enough to adopt out. That someone: Gary.

Finally, Wuffy had her chance. "As soon as she was allowed, she settled herself among the kittens and started licking them—fronts, backs, bellies—the dog was doing my job for me in her own way." That night, she whimpered to wake Gary up every couple of hours: "Time to feed the kittens."

Wuffy was spayed, but Gary is sure she would have produced milk if she could have. "She let the kittens bite at her with those very sharp teeth! She tolerated everything." Between Wuff and Gary, "the kittens all did fine. I was really surprised."

So, an unlikely surrogate mom saves a litter of kitties—it makes for a sweet story. But Wuff was no one-trick pony. She was heroic in both the intensity and the scale of her mothering: She would eventually care for hundreds of different kittens and cats. A friend of Gary's, who worked with a rescue organization, began bringing animals over for Wuff to tend, with Gary's reluctant okay. A sick kitten? Just one? Sure, bring it by. A pair that was abused and needs to learn trust? Okay, we'll give it a try. A litter of four that aren't thriving? Well, I suppose Wuffy can help. Over and over, struggling cats got better under Wuffy's care, eating, playing, and growing strong. "She even taught them how to use the litter box and how to drink from the water bowl. She guarded them, cleaned them, stimulated them." Even one very mean kitten who hissed and bit and swatted at Wuffy was soon tucked into the dog's bed . . . with the dog.

Other organizations across California began calling Gary, asking him to take on other cat cases. Fortunately Gary worked from home, but he admits it became difficult to get his real job done with all the animals about. "We often had four or five babies at a time."

For years, Wuffy was committed to her self-assigned work. Gary guesses she "rescued" 500 to 700 cats and kittens. "It was her reason to live," he says. "When there wasn't a kitten around, she would get depressed. She seemed fulfilled only when she was doing her job."

Though he, too, was instrumental in all the cats' care, Gary gives Wuffy all the credit for the hundreds of success stories. "This was not my calling. It was hers. She would have done it all herself if she could have."

Her last efforts went toward giving cats love at a Siamese rescue organization. When she finally passed away, she was an impressive seventeen and a half years of age. Gary attributes her long life to her warm temperament and to her commitment to something beyond chewing bones and chasing postmen. "So many cats benefited from her, and people, too," he says.

"She is now the heavenly hound," Gary says. "Everybody misses her." Since Wuff died, Gary has stepped down as kitty surrogate. Considering his early cat aversion, he feels he's done more than his part for the feline cause.

IT'S RAINING

One explanation for the phrase "raining cats and dogs" combines the image of Odin, the Norse god who was often pictured with dogs and wolves (symbols of wind), with that of witches on brooms with black cats (symbols of heavy rain). Hence, the phase may refer to a windy rainstorm.

The Loving Llama

AT A REHAB CENTER FOR THE ELDERLY IN OREGON, eighty-nine-year-old Helen is trying hard to sit up in her bed. She rarely makes the effort because it causes her pain and exhausts her. But today is different, and a nurse helps prop her against two pillows so she can see all around. Down the hall, Harold, a usually grouchy guy who hasn't spoken to his fellow residents in months, is feeling chatty. And then there's Grace: Alzheimer's has turned an intelligent spitfire of a woman into a silent shell perched in a chair. But she's reaching out her arms, smiling. She, like the others, just wants to put her hands on Rojo. She sheds a few tears when he arrives, so happy he's come back to see her.

Rojo seems to carry a light within him. He draws you in. His rich reddish coat is so gloriously touchable and comforting that you want to cling to his neck and bury your face in his mane. This animal—a llama—lives to make people feel better. He does it heroically, every day, and everyone who meets him is uplifted by his presence.

Rojo is one of the therapy animals at Mountain Peaks Therapy Llamas and Alpacas (MPTLA), located in Vancouver, Washington. "He was born with a very unusual personality for a llama," says Lori Gregory, president and CEO of MPTLA. "He's so mellow and tolerant."

He was the first llama Lori ever owned. She got him for her daughter who, as a girl, trained and showed Rojo, winning many awards. But that was just the beginning.

Llamas, Lori explains, are smarter than horses and as trainable as dolphins and maybe even dogs. "But you can't coddle them when they're young," she warns. "If you treat them like a buddy early on, they think you're a llama, too, and they'll do what comes naturally—try to dominate you."

But mother and daughter were fortunate to have some great mentors who helped them turn Rojo into a sweetheart. It didn't take much; sweetness was in him already. Once they realized what a gentle beast he was, they decided to share him with people in need.

In need of what? Love. Kindness. Serenity. A laugh. A hug. A

Spreading joy.

soft place to rest their weary heads. The turning point for Lori, what made her decide to take Rojo's training to a higher level, was seeing how the animal affected a young wheelchair-bound boy at a fair. As she writes on the Mountain Peaks website: "A woman came by the llama area, pushing her sweet little boy in his wheelchair. The boy . . . had no hands or feet . . . and I could see his little bald head under his sideways baseball cap. I assured her that Rojo was totally safe for her son to pet, and so she pushed him right up, almost into Rojo's chest hair. As that little guy twirled his arms into Rojo's fiber, his face lit up with a huge smile, and he shouted, 'Mama, I petted a llama! I petted a llama!'"

Seeing his joy, Lori recalls realizing what a gift she had in Rojo. Here was an animal that few had encountered before, so there were no preconceived notions, no bad experiences to overcome. And he made people happy, even those whose lives were a struggle.

Now as a trained therapy animal, Rojo mostly spends time with sick children and the elderly—he's done more than 500 visits so far. He even goes to a local college during final exams, to help students manage their stress. "One of the professors there told me she's never seen so many smiles during finals week as when Rojo is around," says Lori.

Rojo has given much love to kids with autism and with other special cognitive and emotional needs. Some are scared at first, Lori says: He is, after all, 5 foot 6 and some 400 pounds—a bit intimidating. "But now kids that used to hide want to touch him, hug him, walk him on the lead. Some even write poems to him."

One young man, Chris, has struggled with physical and psychological challenges all his life. He's now twenty years old, in adult day care, and doesn't speak. "On our first visit, he would hardly touch Rojo, and didn't want to be near him," Lori recalls. "The

Rojo, lover of hugs and costumes.

second time, he petted him but then ran out of the room. But on the third visit, he came over, cupped Rojo's face in his hands, and stared into his eyes." Always on the lookout for predators, llamas tend to jerk away if their faces are touched or their vision blocked. But Rojo was relaxed, so Chris was, too. "We watched the man transform. It wasn't a verbal thing, but we could see it so clearly."

Accepting intimacy from people isn't most llamas' thing. But for Rojo, it was okay from the start. "He's the only one I know that will let you walk up and throw your arms around him," Lori says. "In general, the animals don't like their backs and lower bodies touched, but with him everything is touchable, even his feet and tail. Kids braid his tail and he doesn't mind. He loves the attention."

The llama is even comfortable in costume. Lori dresses him up for holidays and sometimes elderly residents who rarely come out of their rooms will emerge to see what the llama is wearing. "They get such a kick out of it," Lori says.

She may be slightly biased, she admits, but "Rojo is truly a hero in the way he is able to bring out the joy in everybody. He takes people's minds off their pain. He helps troubled kids to focus on something other than fear and teaches them to trust. When kids are allowed to lead him around, they feel empowered. His kind nature, his acceptance of people, does so much good."

Back at the nursing home, the residents are all smiles as the llama makes rounds. The grumpy guy, on seeing Rojo, softens like butter, then protests when Lori says she has to move on. As she finally leads the animal away, the man follows on his scooter, saying the llama's visit is the best thing that's ever happened there. "The staff says they wish Rojo could come every day," Lori says. "He makes little miracles happen."

A Veteran's Best Friend

LON HODGE'S VOICE GETS TIGHT WHEN HE TALKS ABOUT his losses, about the traumatic events he witnessed as a soldier during the Vietnam War. He is vague about much of his experience, leaving out details that have, for better or worse, shaped his life.

A military "brat" following in his dad's boot steps, Lon joined the army in the early 1970s. He spent a long time working as a counselor to burn victims, and later he was put on bomb disposal. Not surprisingly, Lon saw "terrible, terrible things" (he leaves it at that). "Those things just got bigger and bigger," he says of their effects on him. "I stopped sleeping, began having panic attacks—sometimes five a day. It was like having multiple heart attacks."

And this was before much psychiatric counseling was available to help soldiers soldier on. "No one talked about this stuff back then," he says. "We just didn't discuss it."

Then Lon lost his father to battlefield injuries, and his mother became severely ill. Lon was not only mired in other people's traumas, but his own painful experiences were clawing away at his insides. His energy faded to nothing. "I'd been outdoorsman of the year in the eighties, was a long-distance runner, a black belt in tae kwon do. Then suddenly I couldn't do anything anymore."

Lon's mental state finally hit bottom, and the military put him on medications that, instead of helping, "lobotomized me for a decade. I couldn't think."

But Lon was a fighter. He realized he

From the dock to the doctor, Gander is always by Lon's side.

Gander, a poodle mix, is not your typical service dog.

had to get off the drugs and get his life in order, and soon he began an upward journey. His first boost came from an unlikely source, a stray cat he found while on an extended stay in China. "There were lots of stray animals in the complex where I lived, and one of them started to come to me when she heard my footsteps. We'd just hang out together. It felt good.

"I called her my service cat," he says. "One day she was missing for a few days, then came back and was doing the cat version of the Lassie thing, meowing and running, meowing and running. She had hidden her kittens under a car and was trying to show me. It blew me away! She wouldn't let anyone else near them, but I could pick them up. It was great."

The experience got Lon thinking that if a cat could make him feel so good, maybe a dog would really help him to heal, mentally and physically. So, back in the States, he started looking into dogs for veterans. He came across a group called Freedom Service Dogs, which trains canines to help people with mobility and psychiatric issues. And rather quickly, a special rescue dog became available. It wasn't a lab or a shepherd, as he'd expected. It was a poodle mix.

"When I heard that I thought, oh, so much for my having a macho image!" Lon laughs. But then he heard about how beloved the pup had been during training. "He was the star of the show. People who worked with him cried when he graduated." Lon was won over.

And what a lucky thing that was, he now says.

Lon is sixty years old. Gander is four. "Having him quickly made me realize how internally focused I'd been. I had become so selfish, so self-absorbed. It was by necessity, but I didn't want to be like that anymore." The best way to overcome that, he says, is "to have to get off your butt and take care of someone else. Here was this wonderful loving animal that wants to be touched and played with. It makes you responsible, it makes you think outside of yourself."

With Gander, Lon became more mobile and less isolated. The dog helps with the basics—picking up a credit card or money that Lon drops (without slobbering on them!), opening doors, turning lights on and off. Plus, "he has a sixth sense, knowing when things aren't right for me. If it's too loud, he'll coax me to move to a quieter place," says Lon. "He's so expressive and spot on about everything. Everyone who gets to know him says this is no dog, this is a sophisticated being."

Most important for Lon, "He doesn't ever leave my side."

Lon doesn't have panic attacks anymore, or night terrors (waking up not knowing where he is and what he's doing). "Gander settled a lot of that down." Meanwhile, having the dog has reduced Lon's blood pressure, which used to be sky-high. "I've been able to go off most of my medications," Lon marvels.

POST-TRAUMATIC STRESS DISORDER (PTSD)

An estimated 13 to 20 percent of veterans returning from the wars in Iraq and Afghanistan have PTSD. Studies and personal accounts show that companion dogs may be the best medicine, as they help ease anxiety and depression.

Sure, he says, dogs can be trained to do much of what Gander does. But there's more going on with his pup than just following orders. "I don't have to reward him for anything. It's intuitive. My wife jokes that Gander and I knew each other from other lives, our relationship is so special. He goes above and beyond the call in gentleness, love, and compassion. When he has concern on his face and leans against someone in trauma, that's something really exceptional. That's heroism. He just knows what to do."

There are accidental heroes, Lon says, "and some are instinctively made for this service, heroes from the start." I know Lon is stroking Gander's head and looking into those puppy-dog eyes when he says, "That's this guy."

The Real Energizer Bunny

LIFE IS HARD ENOUGH WHEN YOU ARE BORN WITH PER-fectly working parts. When something is twisted or cracked or missing, life becomes a whole new kind of challenge. It means adapting to a world set up without you in mind. It can be a painful struggle, especially for little kids, who simply want to run and skip, twirl and fall and jump right up again.

When Riki Yahalom Arbel began her career as an animal-assisted therapist in Jerusalem, she wanted to help broken kids to feel whole. And along the way, she found an unlikely partner in her efforts.

Alyna was the tiniest rabbit in a litter of nine at a petting zoo. "At the beginning, I couldn't see that anything was different about

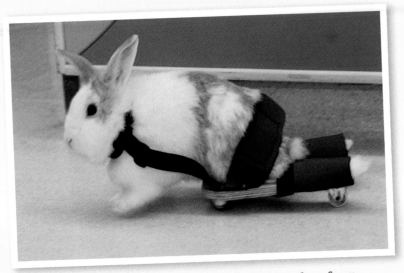

Alyna doesn't let her disability stop her from racing through the hospital.

her," Riki says. "New bunnies are all tucked into the nest and you don't really handle them or see them very well." But once the babies began moving around more freely, Riki noticed that one of them was dragging its back legs. Sadly, those legs were paralyzed.

Riki was amazed that the rabbit was alive, and thriving. "Most of the time, when a mother animal sees something is wrong with a baby, she'll throw it out of the nest." It sounds harsh, but animals in the wild need to save their energy and resources for the young likeliest to survive. Yet this little rabbit's difference had either gone unnoticed or didn't worry the mother very much. Also Alyna was feisty, a trait that may have concealed her disability.

"She was so motivated, right from the start," Riki says. "She would run around the cage despite her legs. She was always first to get food, first to do everything. She was quick and so tough!" Here was an animal who intended to thrive despite her disability. She seemed not to know anything was wrong.

Riki started taking Alyna to work—at ALYN children's hospital, a pediatric and adolescent rehab facility in Israel. There, she noticed a problem. The rabbit's little rear legs weren't indestructible, and they couldn't handle all the dragging around in her cage. Wounds began to appear and Riki worried about infection. She knew that if Alyna were going to survive, she'd need special care— and some kind of contraption to let her move around safely.

"Fortunately, at ALYN, there is a great lab that makes equipment for disabled kids. I went to the lab head, Ohad Gal-Dor, and said hey, I have this rabbit that needs a custom brace. You can imagine his first reaction. He thought I was crazy."

But Riki brought Alyna in and the unusual rabbit quickly won Ohad over. With help from one of the physiotherapists on staff, Riki and Ohad came up with a design for an RGO, or reciprocating gait orthosis, that would suit Alyna's needs. It took a few tries, some special-order wheels that spun in all directions, and various prototypes made with parts recycled from old equipment. Finally, they got it just right.

At first, little Alyna wasn't thrilled to be strapped onto her new scooter, and it took some time for her to understand how to use it. "But once she got the hang of it, she started rolling really fast!" says Riki. "She was pulling herself with her front legs and just racing around. She seemed really happy."

And that's when Riki had a fantastic idea. Alyna, in her scooter, could provide a special service to the hospital in return for the help she'd received there. Riki works with plenty of paralyzed kids, including some who have spina bifida, a birth defect that affects the spinal cord. They may need walking aides or wheelchairs, and they work through a lot of physiotherapy. And here was this rabbit, disabled, just as they were. She couldn't walk and couldn't be potty trained—others had to help keep her clean. "Alyna was truly one of them," Riki says. "And she was working hard with her unique body and her special equipment, like they all have to do. What a great motivator she could be for them."

Soon after Riki's epiphany, Alyna became part of the everyday world of the hospital. The rabbit would zoom down the hospital halls on her new wheels (with her belly down and back legs strapped in, her vehicle was much like the RGO brace many of the kids use), accepting treats and caresses, helping patients to forget their pain and why they were there.

While not all rabbits are keen to be cuddled, this one, called a lion's head rabbit, loved when the young patients stroked her long, silky white-and-brown hair and nuzzled her neck. When Alyna was around, Riki says, "there was a lot of laughing and giggling, and any time a new patient came in, he or she would have this great surprise of seeing the rabbit rolling through."

Most important, as the kids struggled with their therapies, hospital staff would remind them that Alyna didn't like her therapy either—initially she kicked and wiggled when the nurses would strap on her wheels—but she got better with practice, and it was clear to all how much her life improved with her new mobility. So the young patients worked harder, to be more like Alyna. "Talking to them about Alyna's struggles seemed to help the kids feel less afraid and less frustrated. They really felt that Alyna understood them. They could see her doing what they were doing, could tell she, too, was uncomfortable sometimes, so they trusted her."

Over the years, kids wrote her letters and drew pictures of her, to thank her for being such a good friend. She had influenced hundreds of children, showing them how strong they could be, making their rocky paths seem a bit less daunting. After all, there was a little bunny on the same road, wheeling along beside them.

ANIMALS DO GOOD

Studies show that traumatized or troubled children who undergo animal-assisted therapy (AAT) have lower blood pressure, less anxiety, and higher self-esteem and are more comfortable opening up to people. Often, they open up to the animal first.

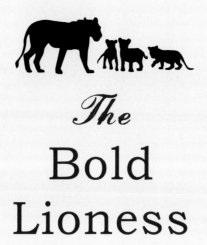

The
Bold
Lioness

LIFE IN THE WILD IS A PRECARIOUS THING. **D**ANGER hangs like a dark cloud even on the sunniest days. For a photographer in that environment, staying alert and ready to act is the key to success—to getting that jaw-dropping shot of something rarely seen. But, for the animals, such readiness means nothing less than survival. It separates those who live from those who die.

There's a natural haven in Botswana called the Okavango Delta, where water is life. Annual flooding transforms lands to lakes and canals, and wildlife thrives on the riches. It's the perfect environment for a photographer like Pia Dierickx of Belgium to catch wild animals in the act of doing wild things.

The lioness springs into action, pounces on the croc, and scares off the predator.

A few years ago, Pia and a small group of friends spent seventeen days in the delta chasing the perfect light, their lenses trained on whatever animals crept into view. And during that trip, they witnessed—and Pia captured on film—a thrilling scene that surely happens every day, but that to us seems as heroic as a person rushing into a burning house to save a child.

The group had stopped to shoot photos of an African rock python, but realizing there was a pride of lions nearby keeping their eyes on the human interlopers, they returned to their vehicle. They drove on at a crawl, looking for a beautiful and safe spot to stop for a break. Then they saw a lone lioness up ahead. "She was sniffing the ground, presumably looking for the remainder of her pride," Pia says. "We moved closer to investigate. And suddenly there they were, all eighteen of them, the entire pride of lions in view. They were moving with great intent toward a shallow channel where vultures were feeding on a carcass."

Lions in the Okavango aren't like house cats; they can't shy away from water, because lunch may be on the other side. Still, they don't relish swimming and take great care before crossing, "often growling, snarling, and testing the water with their paws," Pia says. The water itself doesn't appeal to them and, more important, even these top predators have enemies and must be on their guard when out of their element.

But with food uppermost on their minds, two of the lionesses walked straight into the channel, eyes on the vulture-covered carcass ahead rather than on the surrounding water. And that's when the crocodile revealed itself, it's long leathery snout and glaring eyes showing above the surface. "The first lioness didn't see the croc but the second one might have," Pia recalls. Oddly, though, "she didn't react and simply continued to follow the other cat"—perhaps too hungry to consider the risk fully.

CRASHING LIONS

Lions greet one another by rubbing against each other to exchange scents. Sometimes the collision is so forceful, one or both of the lions fall down. Still, much of the time these big cats are "lazy" (really just conserving energy), sleeping up to 20 hours a day.

The crocodile moved swiftly to the deeper water, she recalls, and set itself up just in front of the second lioness. Still, the cat was either unaware or unconcerned about this reptile in their midst. And then, quick as a lightning strike, the croc made its move. Powering through the water, it flew toward its potential prey, jaws snapping. That big cat was in trouble.

But rather than fleeing, the lioness, now fully aware of what lay before her, responded with great strength. She rose up like a regal warrior, facing down her foe. And despite how things began, the cat would now prove victorious, scaring off the croc before it could harm her or any of the other lions that were now entering the channel. The whole thing was over in just seconds, but that lioness had saved the day.

During the face-off, "she sounded a call that I have never

Protector of the pride.

heard before," Pia says, a sort of growling alarm, a wild battle cry. "The remaining females in the pride came running toward the commotion," but it was already over, the crocodile having moved quickly downstream. And shortly, the rest of the pride finished moving across the channel in small groups. Some were just cubs, and would have been especially vulnerable to the croc's snapping jaws. But with her protective stand, the lioness had made the crossing safe.

The heroic big cat was of course protecting herself, an automatic response, survival of the fittest. But as a sister, a daughter, and perhaps a mother to some of the cubs in the pride, the animal did a great deed in standing up to the predatory croc. One lion's natural behavior served the entire group, perhaps saving more lives than her own and clearing the way for her family to feed in peace.

The treacherous crossing looks benign.

The Therapeutic Goat

SARA MANLEY GREW UP STEEPED IN THE DUSTY, SWEET smells and neigh-and-baa chorus of the farm. Not the best environment to be in if you have respiratory problems, perhaps, but Sara never let terrible allergies stop her from spending time on her relatives' Texas property. "I've had to strive and suffer to be around the things I love," she says. Allergies aren't her only challenge—Sara suffers from a rare autoimmune disorder, spinal problems, and muscular seizures. Her blood sugar drops quickly as a result of her medications, and that, too, can cause spasms, seizures, or even blackouts. She also has a bad leg that sometimes won't support her weight.

Despite it all, Sarah can ride horses—a big passion of hers.

So she rescued one, and boarded it at a dairy goat farm near where she lives in Michigan. And there she became smitten with these other hoofed creatures. The goats were smart and funny, and they were drawn to her. In fact, she noticed that sometimes the animals seemed to know before she did that she was going to have a seizure. "They'd get so fired up; I honestly felt I'd done something to upset them," she says. But she saw a pattern in their strange behavior: Their cries and sudden biting seemed to signal an impending episode of ill health.

Sara decided that such an animal would be a great companion for her. At the goat farm, there was an orphan goat who also had a long list of troubles, just like she did, and she bonded with him from day one. "He was very sick at birth and his mother rejected him," Sara says. "We had to tube-feed him for the first week of his life," and bottle-feed him for a while after. Prince, as she called him, got better under her care, and soon Sara noticed that he had a special awareness of her condition, even more than the other goats had shown. "At just three weeks of age, he was showing signs of sensing my low blood sugar and muscular seizures," she says. "He would nip, scream, and run around to get my attention, and I began rewarding him," so he got better and better at it.

She spoiled the animal a little: He slept in bed with her in his own little pajamas. She also "bomb-proofed" him so he'd be calm in public. "A lot of goats are skittish, so I would drive him around

Prince can sense Sara's low blood sugar and muscular seizures.

in the car, blasting metal music to get him used to loud noises."
Her purpose was to certify Prince as an official therapy animal—
a goal that the two of them soon reached.

Scientists don't completely understand why some animals
are so sensitive to human disorders. Probably they are tuned in
to unusual smells; many diseases have a signature scent that we
humans aren't typically able to recognize but that other animals
can detect. Usually, an animal needs to be trained to respond to a
new scent, though you'd be surprised at how many species can do
it naturally. Even honeybees can learn to signal when they catch a

Prince's calm demeanor is contagious.

whiff of a specific odor. And reports by animal owners of spontaneous responses, often warnings that something smells wrong, aren't uncommon.

Prince, then, was one of the spontaneous detectors. After Sara worked to reinforce the behavior, Prince learned that it was his job to warn Sara of any oncoming problems. "He will also guard me if I fall down," she says. "When he's older, he'll also help with my stability issues—I have severe nerve damage in both legs— and he'll be able to carry a forty-pound pack" on hikes, horseback rides, and shopping trips. In return, Prince gets a lot of love and rubs, and delicious grain pellets and animal crackers. He's a big hit in public and seems to revel in the attention.

Prince usually stays at the farm where he was born, living part time as a "normal" goat. But when he's with Sara, he works, making her life a whole lot easier and more fun. "He's my little hero," she says. "He keeps me safe outdoors, and he makes me laugh and definitely feel loved. He reminds me not to take things so seriously. He has a 'been there, done that' calmness about him that calms me and everyone around him."

OLD GOAT

Goats were some of the first animals to be domesticated, bred, and herded by humans in the Near East at least 10,000 years ago. Now there are more than 200 different breeds around the world giving milk, meat, leather, and fiber—and companionship—to people.

The goat has also taught Sara that medications and physical therapy aren't the answers to everything, and she's accepted that some questions, whether about her own health or about the goat's special abilities, may just be unanswerable. "And that's okay."

Sara spoils Prince a bit. "He snuggles with me on the couch," she admits. "And he likes his popcorn with butter."

The little Prince.

A
Canine
in the Clouds

SOME DOGS PLAY FETCH. **O**THERS ROLL OVER OR SLAP a paw in your hand on command, or stand on their hind legs for treats.

This dog flies.

Shadow was just a pup when Dan McManus brought him home. Dan himself was a troubled guy at the time, having suffered early on from unfocused anxiety and ADD, and later experiencing night terrors and serious panic attacks. He wasn't just home from a war, hadn't suffered an obvious trauma, but his fears were deeply rooted and very real. And they were becoming more and more debilitating as he aged. He was finally diagnosed with bipolar disorder.

Dan had found one thing that seemed to keep him on an even keel—hang gliding. He'd first tried the sport back in the 1970s and was quickly hooked. He now owns a hang gliding business in Utah. He says that when he is soaring above the land, the sun and wind rinsing his face clean, his worries become specks like the people below him. He is able to leave it all behind, to feel alive.

But he has to touch down eventually. And for a long time whenever his feet hit the ground, Dan's agony returned. He started reading up on psychiatric service animals. "I remembered as a kid when I'd spend time outside with dogs, sleeping with them in the yard, I'd be so comfortable," Dan says. "Those memories made me realize a dog was what I needed." He finally asked his doctor to prescribe a therapy dog to help him function. The animal would stay by his side all the time, helping to keep his owner's anxiety in check.

Shadow is an Australian cattle dog, and he is literally Dan's constant companion. "There's no leaving this guy alone," says Dan. "He suffers from a little anxiety of his own, separation anxiety, so I take him everywhere." And that was the whole idea, after all. Man and dog bonded very quickly, really on the first day they met. And Shadow was easily trained on the skills he needed to meet therapy-dog criteria—the obedience and "good canine citizen" behaviors that would allow him into public buildings, buses, and the like.

Dan and Shadow on a hang gliding trip.

The rest, though—the "therapy" part—came naturally. "Shadow immediately started doing things for me, and having a calming effect on me even before I realized it," Dan says. And over time, the dog has become even more attuned to his owner's needs. "If I am having a night terror, he'll wake me up before the heart attack–like symptoms kick in. If I start to feel panicky in the car, he'll get in my lap and I'll realize I need to get off the road." And if Dan is part of a crowded gathering, he says, "Shadow just sits quietly and watches me. If he sees me getting antsy, he'll walk over and I'll pet him, which calms me down."

And then there's the flying thing. Shadow, like Dan, seems

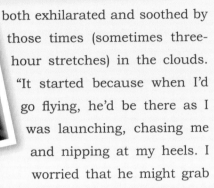

both exhilarated and soothed by those times (sometimes three-hour stretches) in the clouds. "It started because when I'd go flying, he'd be there as I was launching, chasing me and nipping at my heels. I worried that he might grab my harness and end up getting hurt if he let go. I knew I had to break him of the habit." But rather than restrain the dog on flying days, Dan built him a special heavy-duty harness of his own, so Shadow, too, could fly. "It's very safe—there's no way for him to get out of it," he says. Dan tested Shadow in the harness at home, strapping him in, putting him on his back, and swinging him around to see how he'd react. "It didn't bother him at all."

Shadow is Dan's copilot, in life and in the sky.

So, not surprisingly, "he was super happy the first time we went up," Dan says. And like a kid at a carnival, the dog just wanted to ride *one more time*. "So, back into the harness, back into the sky we went," Dan says. The dog, when he's tucked in tightly behind his owner, puts his front legs around Dan and does a sort of canine meditation. "He just hangs out back there, smelling the smells and looking around, watching birds, very relaxed. He seems to know what's going on. He even shifts his weight with me when I need to turn. He's really learned what to do."

The joint flights didn't break Shadow of his habit of chasing Dan on solo flights, but that has now become a manageable game. Dan will deliber-

BRAINY DOG

Another Australian cattle dog, Skidboot, often called the world's smartest dog, helped his owner with his horseshoeing business until they were discovered and took their show on the road. Skidboot made appearances on the *Oprah Winfrey Show* and *Late Night With David Letterman*.

ately fly low, over Shadow's head, to rile him up. And the dog always recognizes him, knowing which glider is his, even when there are many others landing on the same hill. "When I land, he's always right there, waiting for me. It's great for both of us."

"Shadow . . . takes care of me," Dan says. "People get tired of asking and hearing about how you're feeling, especially if they can't relate to it. But I know Shadow is there to sit with me, to play ball, to lick my face, or give a little extra love. He simply makes me feel better, which is a huge victory for me, and you really can't train a dog to do that." Shadow is Dan's valiant copilot, in life and also in the sky. "Flying with him brings together the two constants in my life, and that's the best therapy there is."

Jesse Knott
with Koshka in
Afghanistan.

The
Infantry Kitty

"IN WAR, THERE ARE NO UNWOUNDED SOLDIERS,"
penned Argentine writer José Narsky for a Veterans Day
speech in 2010. It's a truth well known to people like Jesse Knott.
Jesse joined the military in 2006, after hearing the story of a
marine in Fallujah who, during an ambush, abandoned cover to
search for a friend. "I thought, I should be there, doing something," he says. He chose the army's infantry—the "boots on the
ground" soldiers—because "if I was going to do it, I was going to do
it all the way." And now he can speak to both the physical wounds
and the deep emotional scars that war leaves behind.

He will also tell you that during wartime, the littlest forms
of pleasure are true gifts. His own gift, which held him together

during the worst moments of his life, was a scrappy little feral kitten. If there is a feline war hero, Jesse says, it is Koshka.

During his first tour of duty in Iraq, Jesse was injured by a roadside bomb. But that didn't keep him from heading to Afghanistan with his men

Koshka was "the mascot" for Jesse's company.

in 2010. And it was at a tiny faraway outpost near a town called Maywan that Koshka entered his world.

"I grew up with cats, and always loved them," Jesse says. When he first arrived in Maywan, he noticed a few around the base, kindly keeping the mouse and rat populations under control. One in particular, a green-eyed tiger kitten, took to Jesse—maybe because of the meat snacks and chin scratches the soldier offered up. For Jesse, the animal was a delightful distraction.

Someone had been mistreating the kitten. One day, Jesse noticed sore spots where the cat had been nicked by a razor, and another day, it was limping on a torn toe pad, leaving a bloody trail behind. He was appalled and angry. With his eye out for the culprit, he took the cat in to care for it himself. Because of his earlier injuries, he had been assigned to work on intelligence projects, which meant he had an office—the perfect place to keep his pet.

"I marveled that this wild little thing let me hold him on his back to work on his injuries," Jesse says. The cat, which he eventually named Koshka (meaning "kitty," fondly, in Russian) proved to be really smart. "He even let me know that he needed a litter box—mewing and scratching at the door rather than making a mess in the office." (Jesse made one with a box lid and some sand from outdoors.) "Here was this feral cat quickly acting very domesticated. All I really wanted to do was to get him out of there, to send him home so he'd be safe," Jesse explains.

Feral animals weren't really allowed at the camp anyway. Jesse found an organization in Kabul, the Afghan Stray Animal League, that would be willing to take Koshka and help ship him to the States, but first the cat had to get to Kabul. Whenever a helicopter landed on base with supplies, Jesse tried to sweet-talk the crew into taking the cat aboard for a trip to the capital city. But it wasn't an easy sell.

And then came tragic

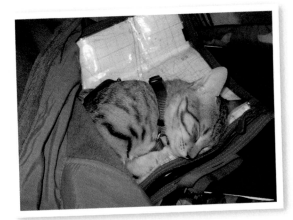

The kitten was a cheerful presence for soldiers.

Koshka and Jesse in Oregon.

news—news that would send Jesse to a very dark place. "That December, two of my men, my friends, were killed by a suicide bomber. I lost it. I felt . . . done. I couldn't handle it and truly wanted to check out. I had a plan and everything. I wanted to die."

Koshka was with Jesse on this horrible day. As Jesse's emotions took hold of him, the cat sensed his friend's distress and seemed to know what to do. "He kept coming up and head-bonking me—he wouldn't leave me alone," Jesse recalls. "And he was purring. I'd never heard him do that before. He kept patting my face with his paw, swiping me with his tail, and then he curled up in my lap, rumbling away. It was enough to pull me back to my senses, back to reality, to realize I can't do this to myself. I've got other responsibilities. I need to pull it together."

"He saved my life that night," Jesse says. "I have no doubt about that. And after that, it became my mission to get him out of that country, no matter what."

In the meantime, Koshka continued to help other soldiers as well.

"He was amazing. We had soldiers dragging themselves back from patrols—they would have been out in horrible heat walking with one hundred pounds of gear for six hours—and before going to their rooms, they'd come by and play with the cat. Koshka became a mascot for our company. Everybody loved coming by to see him."

"You develop a hardness when you're deployed during war," Jesse continues. "It becomes evident in your eyes and heart. But I'd watch soldiers playing with this kitten and see smiles creep in, warmth come back to their eyes. The effect of this cute little animal was enormous. It felt fabulous to give something back to these soldiers, to remind them that there's more to life than what they're experiencing right now."

After endless calls, Jesse found an interpreter who was taking a dog to Kabul and agreed to carry Koshka, too. It was a long trip on buses and planes. But finally Koshka made it to Kabul, then to New York, and lastly to Jesse's parents' home in Oregon.

"When I saw how happily he bonded with my parents, how much they cared about him, we decided he could stay there," Jesse says. And Koshka, the cat who saved the soldier with his perfectly timed purr, remains in Oregon today—a contented, much-loved pet living the kitty version of the American dream.

Big-Picture Heroes

Doing Good Stuff Now, for Later

"Heroes give hope."

—*Amit Kalantri*

THESE ARE THE ANIMALS WHO UNKNOWINGLY CONTRIBUTE TO the bigger picture, whether by bringing attention to unexpected capabilities that can serve people later, or by being part of a conservation cause. They are heroes of another sort, but heroes just the same.

Toola snuggles with an orphan pup.

The

Sea Otter Supermoms

AS YOU READ THIS, SEA OTTERS ARE FLOATING AROUND off the coasts of California, Washington, Alaska, Canada, and Russia. A few might be basking near Japan. These sweet-faced, densely furred marine mammals, which are related to badgers and weasels, used to range widely in the North Pacific Ocean. But otter pelts are warm and luxurious, and they shed water. So sea otters were hunted by seafaring adventurers starting in the mid-1700s, and by the early 1900s their populations were almost gone. Now, despite longtime legal protection, the southern group off the coast of California still numbers only 2,900 animals where at least 20,000 used to live. (The northern population is stronger, with maybe 80,000. Still, there used to be more than 1 million sea otters.)

Joy (left), "the consummate mom."

So, staff who work with otters at the Monterey Bay Aquarium in California have been testing ways to keep the southern group from slipping away. It's been a learn-as-they-go program. Some failures, some victories. But by saving and healing stranded animals and bringing new ones into the world, they're working to create the blueprints for a program that, eventually, will help the population to grow.

Elkhorn Slough is a 7-mile-long tidal marsh and estuary north of Monterey Bay. Calm waters and lots of clams, crabs, and other tasty invertebrates make this a heaven for sea otters, so it is a natural place to drop off healthy animals and monitor their progress. For years, before letting young otters go, biologists acted as otter parents—actually taking pups offshore and attempting to teach them how to dive down and collect seafood. They tried hard, but they knew baby otters do best with mother otters for teachers.

That's in part because otter pups need lots of adult attention. They are born utterly helpless, and like corks bobbing on the surface of the water, they have no real control over their movements. Two otter moms named Toola and Joy, the heroes in this tale, were able to show the biologists how proper otter mothering is done.

The surrogacy program began with a two-week-old male otter who stranded (came ashore in distress) in Monterey Bay back in 2001. Toola was the first mom asked to take on a baby not her own. She, too, had stranded, and the aquarium had taken her in to find out why. She had a nasty parasite that required lifelong treatment, and that meant she couldn't be released back into the wild. She had recently given birth to a stillborn pup (probably also infected), and was swimming around with it in her arms, unwilling to give it up.

Toola waves hello.

But when the tiny, motherless otter pup was placed in her tank, she immediately took to him. She had finally let go of her lifeless baby, and now she let this new pup snuggle in to nurse. He happily drank the milk Toola's body had produced for her own pup. It was the first sign of success.

Hero Mom Number Two: Joy. "Small stature, big heart, bigger attitude," wrote Karl Mayer, the aquarium's animal care coordinator for the Sea Otter Research and Conservation Program, in a newsletter article about this special animal. Joy was herself stranded as just a wee thing, brought into captivity, and raised under the old model—with people teaching her how to be wild— then released. But she was too accepting of people for her own good. She would play with divers and even climb onto surf-boards. The aquarium team tried moving her to remote areas, as much as 80 miles away, but within 48 hours she'd always come back. Finally, she came home to the aquarium for good. It was the end of Joy's term as a wild otter, but the beginning of her special job as a surrogate mom. Between the two moms, more than thirty otter pups were raised, most of them for release into the wild.

What makes a good otter mom? "She'll protect the pup," says Karl. "If confronted with a net, she'll take her baby and try to avoid it. She'll carry the pup on her chest, groom it, and share food with it. And of course she'll allow it to suckle, even if she isn't really producing milk." Joy and Toola watched over each pup for as long as five months.

Joy bonds with a new pup.

Joy seemed to thrive in her parenting role. Karl calls her "the consummate mom." Sometimes she'd take on two babies at once, giving them equal attention. In all, she mothered some twenty pups. "She tolerated whatever we asked of her, and that was a lot. The demands of bonding with even one pup can be considerable," Karl says. Joy wasn't

always easy to work with. One handler, bloodied from trying to separate
Joy from a baby for the day's swim,
called her "a pit bull." But maybe that
fierce protectiveness was just part
of her excellent parenting. After all,
her first adoptee is now eleven years
old, a healthy male holding territory
in Elkhorn Slough. Twelve other Joy
"alumni" have also been released into
the wild.

BIG EATERS

An otter mom uses a vast
store of energy to feed her pup, up
to 133 percent of her body mass! To
make up for it she must hunt for
herself, and may use seaweed to
tether her baby to keep it from
drifting while she's away.

 Toola was wilder in spirit than
Joy, and despite her initial willingness, became more reluctant to
mother orphan pups later on. But she eventually accepted every
baby given to her and protected and cared for them well. "Her
maternal side was solid once she took to a pup," Karl says. Toola's
successes include eleven of thirteen adoptees set free in the slough
since 2001. So far, three of her female protégés (and four of Joy's)
have reared pups in the wild.

 And in the near future, because of what Toola and Joy taught
the aquarium staff, other surrogate otters could help save pups left
behind after a natural or human-caused disaster (like oil spills).
It's one of many ways that these substitute moms do a hero's
labor, keeping their species alive, one furry-faced baby at a time.

Wicket with Zambian wildlife authorities.

The Dogs *Who* Sniff *to* Save Species

WICKET IS A BUNDLE OF ENERGY WRAPPED IN A SOFT, black coat. Her ears and nose twitch, her runner's muscles ripple, but her eyes stay focused on her handler. When she hears the command, Wicket knows what to do. Nose to the ground, the Labrador retriever begins her search, moving efficiently through the leaves, up and back, sniffing. There are plenty of potential distractions, but Wicket ignores them.

Suddenly, she sits, the signal that she's found the target. Aimee Hurt approaches and looks around, but sees nothing. "Where is it, girl?" Aimee asks. Wicket's nose dips back to the ground, and this time when her head comes up there's something sticking to the end of her snout. "It's a rosy wolf snail, about two millimeters long," Aimee says. (That's smaller than a flea.) It's the species they're looking for, an exotic snail that has driven three-quarters of Hawaii's native snails extinct since the 1930s. Such a tiny specimen "was an amazing find," she says.

Sniffer dog Pepin awaits his orders.

Tracking snails may not seem like much of a job. But if you are a conservationist trying to preserve native species and habitats, finding the enemy, whether a snail or something more obviously menacing, is paramount.

And anyway, Wicket's sniffing talent goes well beyond snails. She knows twenty animal and plant scents that have allowed her to help efforts worldwide. She can find grizzly and black bear, wolf, and mountain lion poop. She knows the smell of California's endangered desert tortoise and sniffs out (but doesn't chase!) Franklin's ground squirrels. She's tracked the scent of Asiatic black bear scat in China, and Cross River gorilla dung in Cameroon.

Lily, another conservation hero.

Wicket is part of a group called Working Dogs for Conservation (WDC), based in Three Forks, Montana, of which Aimee is a founder. The group's sniffer dogs typically work two kinds of projects. One kind aims to count the number of animals in a population or find out how they use the landscape—information that helps in resolving conflicts between developers and conservationists. The other project type focuses on exotic species—stuff that lives where it doesn't belong—helping scientists find and get rid of them.

Simply put, dogs home in on poop (and other smells) better and faster and more often than people do. Their noses are tens of thousands of times more sensitive than ours, with scores more olfactory receptors. A dog can separate out one scent from a mix of them, and can zoom in on, say, a bit of scat 30 feet off the trail. A ranger will likely only notice it—by eye—if it's less than 4 feet away. And even among dogs, Wicket is extraordinarily good at her job. "She knows more of these animal scents than any other dog in the program," Aimee says. "And she's always ready to work. She has that drive in abundance."

WDC uses the same processes to train their dogs that are used for drug- or mine-sniffing dogs, with a ball as the reward. "Except we have some special challenges," Aimee explains. "Our dogs work over very long periods, off leash, in natural wild environments. It takes a unique dog to ignore the distractions, and not to harass or injure the wildlife. Among a thousand dogs evaluated, only one will have what it takes to do the job."

Wicket, who was a "crazy" rescue dog when Aimee met her, turned out to be easy to train, enthusiastic, and smart. She's become Aimee's "right-hand man." At least half of the items Wicket has been trained to find are firsts—no dogs have ever tracked them before.

So, what is this dog actually accomplishing with her superior sniffing? Her nose inspired the relocation of a planned development away from a grizzly bear habitat in Montana's Centennial Mountains. In South Africa, she found the exceptionally rare geometric tortoise and located a long-lost female whose transmitter had fallen off. And the dog's efforts not only led to finding kit fox where they hadn't been seen in forty years, but they also pointed out the best kit fox habitat, which the Bureau of Land Management then bought for the animals' protection.

Now Wicket is the leading dog in a brand-new effort. WDC took its dogs to Zambia in Africa to practice tracking down snares— the wild-animal traps that poachers use to catch often-threatened species. Aimee says WDC got real snares from Zambia to use in training. Once in the field, the dogs would learn additional scents associated with the traps—human scents.

But once her nose was on the ground, Wicket went even further. Aimee explains that where snares are hooked into trees, the tree gets wounded, giving off a certain smell. The same is true when twigs and branches are broken after someone tramples them. Without any specific training, "Wicket started cluing in on snapped branches, wounded plants, but not the types broken by elephants. She found combined scents of the metals plus human hands that helped lead us to the snares themselves. It was real detective work!" (It was also a great deterrent for poachers, who heard rumors that the dogs could identify the individuals who set the traps.)

As a final bonus, Wicket befriended the children in the village. "Dogs on the streets there are often kicked and teased, and kids aren't taught to care for them," Aimee says. "So when I invite kids to come pet Wicket or play fetch with her, they see there's another way to interact with animals." Having children learn how to be kind to other creatures? That might just be the best outcome of all.

*Amelie, surrogate
mother, with one of her
black-footed kittens.*

House Cats Gone Wild

IF YOU HAPPEN TO BE LYING ON YOUR BELLY IN THE GRASS-lands of southern Africa, you might glimpse the tiniest feline species on the continent—the black-footed cat—slinking around, hunting rodents and ground-roosting birds. But it's more likely you won't see one. Not only are they quite small (adult females are only around 2 pounds), but they are extremely rare. Perhaps 10,000 wild adults are left in the world, scattered here and there. That might sound like a big number, but when you're talking about an entire species, that's very few indeed.

The problem for this kind of cat is that grazing animals are chewing up its habitat, and people who put out poison for other pest species kill cats by mistake; scientists say cat numbers are going down.

Are there ways to make more of these animals without having to capture lots of wild ones to breed them? It turns out that the method used with humans called in-vitro fertilization (IVF), a controlled way to help a pregnancy get started, can work in cats, too. Scientists at the Audubon Center for Research of Endangered Species, in New Orleans, have found that they can create endangered cat embryos by this method. What they do is collect oocytes (eggs) from a black-footed cat female and transfer them into the womb of a regular house cat. Then they fertilize those eggs with previously frozen sperm from a black-footed cat male. The center can also freeze endangered-cat embryos to use later. In this way, it can make lots of black-footed babies without needing lots of black-footed parents. This is good news for all the smaller rare and vulnerable felines out there that may need a boost in population someday.

At the Audubon Center, two big rooms are outfitted with lots of toys, scratching posts, and soft places for a colony of about 100 domestic cats, all females. Striped, spotted, calico, orange—it's quite a kitty menagerie. Out of all of them, Amelie, a domestic short hair, is the supermom of the bunch. "She's actually a little shy with people, but she's very sweet," says zookeeper Karen Ross. "It takes time for her to learn trust, but once she does, she'll come right up to you. She really likes having her chin scratched." Pretty typical cat, it seems.

In the wild, black-footed kittens live in dens with their mothers.

What's not typical is that Amelie recently gave birth to a perfectly healthy black-footed kitten, Crystal, weighing in at 2.3 ounces—about the size of a generous meatball. And if she noticed that Crystal was a bit "different"—growing bigger and stronger much faster than the usual domestic kitten—that didn't stop her from nursing and caring for the little one for the first few weeks.

At the outset, the two were placed with the rest of the colony, "but we found that the kitten, even before her eyes were open, was stressed by all the activity in the main cat room— she'd hiss and get upset when the keepers came in and out. So we moved Amelie and Crystal into a room by themselves," says senior scientist Earle Pope. "In the wild, black-footed kittens live isolated in a den with mom, so it made sense to give them their own space."

But Amelie was very social among her own kind, and she seemed to want to do her mothering in public. "Amelie figured out how to jump up on the door handle and open the door," Karen

Captive breeding of the black-footed cat (here, in the wild) has been very encouraging.

says. "She's a very smart kitty! We had to start locking the door to make sure the special baby stayed put."

Regardless, "She was a great mother," Earle says. "She raised the kitten without it needing supplemental food, quite a feat."

Eventually the scientists separated the two to protect Amelie from what became an overzealous baby. Also, "exotics eat meat and mice and such, not regular cat food," Karen explains. So after Crystal was weaned, feedings were separate.

Still, the two would play together, and Amelie accepted the wildness in her offspring, tolerating the baby's rough pouncing and biting of ears.

This isn't the very first demonstration of "interspecies procreational compatibility" (big words that simply mean an animal of one species giving birth to healthy babies of another species). That distinction goes to a litter of sand cat kittens born to a domestic cat back in 2008. Later, scientists had similar success using IVF to produce an African wildcat from a house cat's womb.

But what makes this case special is that, unlike the African wildcat, whose population is fairly hearty, the black-footed cat is in trouble, so captive breeding of the species is very important. And with so many big cats in deep trouble (think lions, tigers, cheetahs), Amelie's success as a surrogate is especially encouraging.

Unfortunately, your average house cat can't give birth to lions and tigers; the size difference makes that impossible. But the success of the method means that interspecies surrogacy for this purpose is moving forward.

"This work, what Amelie has done, is a small but important part of the puzzle," Earle says. "If we can continue to make progress with this process, it can play a role in conserving endangered cats and protecting particular genetics that are important to keeping these populations going."

INTERSPECIES PROCREATION

Similar embryo-transfer work has worked well with other kinds of animals. A domestic cow has given birth to a gaur (a wild ox from Southeast Asia), and a common eland (a type of antelope) produced a bongo.

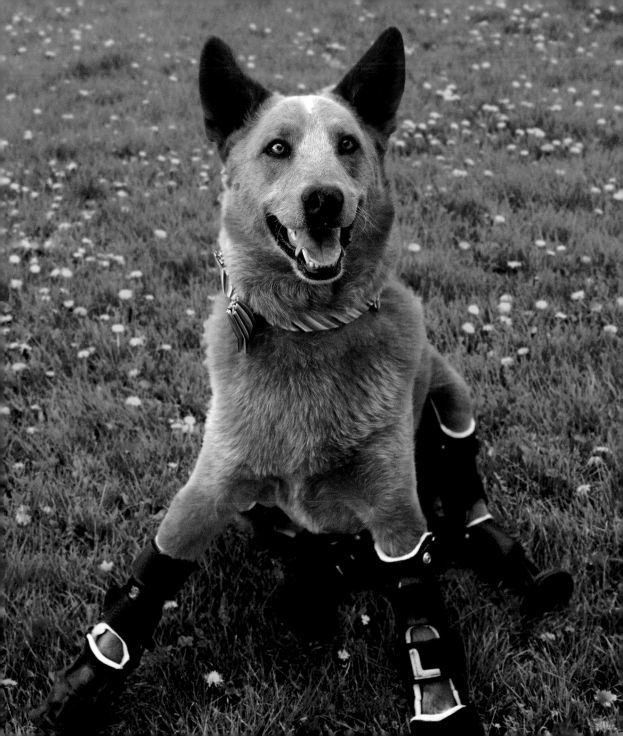

The Bionic Dog

"**T**HERE'S A BIT OF MAGIC IN EVERYTHING, AND SOME loss to even things out." It's a line from a Lou Reed song, and it makes me think about a sweet pup named Naki'o. In Naki'o's case, first came a lot of loss, then just the right amount of magic. Loss returned briefly, then the magic swooped back in. And through it all, this dog held on to his joyous—and yes, heroic—spirit.

As a tiny puppy back in 2010, Naki'o was discovered with his family in the ice-cold basement of a Nebraska home. The owners had fled foreclosure, and their dog was left behind either pregnant or having recently given birth. The mama didn't survive, but when rescuers arrived they found her puppies—red heeler mixed breeds—miraculously still alive and squirming. One of them, though, was in very rough shape, severely frostbitten, his paws held fast to a frozen puddle on the basement floor.

All four feet had to be amputated to save this little dog's life. For an animal built to run and play, such a loss could have been devastating, and might have made the dog undesirable to potential adoptive parents. But then came the first spark of magic.

Christie Pace was scrolling through a pet-finding website when she came across Stubby (as he was then known) and his sad story. "That day, I was really just perusing to get an idea of what kind of dog I might want to adopt, not to actually pick one." But when she saw the photo and read Stubby's history, "I fell in love. I went to see him, and he was all smiles, running on his little stumps and jumping into my lap to kiss me." The dog had also lost a bit of his tail, a nip of nose, and a chunk of ear from the frostbite, but somehow these scars added to his charm. "Of course," says Christie, "I brought him home."

That Stubby was a special-needs dog didn't worry Christie, who was a veterinary technician and was allowed to take him to work with her each day. Plus, he was so joyful, so seemingly unaware of his missing feet and able to maneuver pretty darn well without them. One leg was worse than the others and Christie thought she might have to address it down the line. But for the time being, both she and the dog managed.

As Stubby—whom Christie renamed Naki'o, meaning "puddle" in Hawaiian—grew and his bones took shape, he began to struggle with his disability. (The dog's new name reflected his owner's birthplace, the cause of the pup's injuries, and his "mistakes" during house training.) He also got heavier. "I had to carry him everywhere, put him in the car, help him up the steps," Christie says. "We couldn't really take a walk, and if he was out to play he had to stay on the soft grass. Carrying him was fine when he was little, but by the time he was fifty pounds, it was pretty difficult!" Christie used a stroller and a red wagon to help cart the pup around, but it was slow going. "He didn't like to be left at home. He

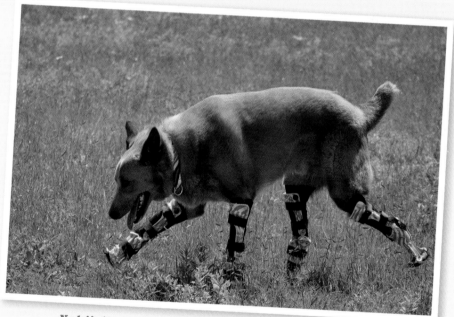

Naki'o's prosthetics are decorated in American flags to pay tribute to veteran amputees.

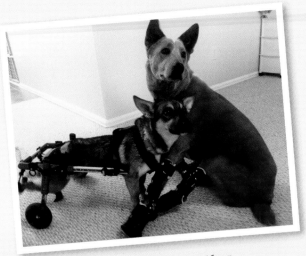
Naki'o inspires other disabled pets.

wanted to be involved with the family all the time."

Still, "he never complained," Christie marvels. "His personality was still great, he was always happy. But there were little signs, behaviors, showing that he was in pain." And soon that pain turned to sores on the most damaged back leg, which Christie worried could become infected. "It was a constant battle with antibiotics, pain medications. We were always soaking his sores, trying to heal them." When Naki'o was one year old and still struggling, Christie knew it was time to try something new.

Christie began researching prosthetics. She heard of a company called OrthoPets that makes custom prosthetics for animals with great success. "It was fate," she says. "They were exactly what I needed. It was a blessing that I came across them."

Raising $1,000 for the first leg was easy. "We put a jar up front at the vet clinic and lots of clients donated. They all knew Naki'o, knew his story, and they'd bonded with him at the clinic. The community really pulled together." Then OrthoPets did a wonderful thing: The company donated the other three prosthetics!

The hind leg prosthetics were made first, one at a time, and Naki'o pretty quickly figured out how to walk around on them. "He became comfortable, was able to play outside and chase balls with less pain."

With that victory, OrthoPets suggested doing both front paws at the same time, to even him out.

The procedure goes like this: First vets do a simple surgery on each leg to clean and smooth the surface of the bone where the prosthetic will go. Then the new legs are cast, with lots of cushioning, to fit the leg nubs perfectly. Each leg nub goes into a socket that closes on it like a clamshell while letting the animal's knee bend above it. Velcro straps and padding hold it in place. The "feet" don't resemble animal paws—the black rubber-bottomed parts seem more apt for a table than a dog, but they hold up to romps and leaps as well as any natural body part does.

And suddenly, the dog with no feet had four on the floor.

"The first time he stood up he was wobbly, like a newborn fawn. Having had no paws, he didn't know where his limbs were in space." But then, says Christie, "he started walking, then running and jumping. He was doing everything he couldn't do before, and loving it. We'd actually take a real walk down the street! That was a great accomplishment, and of course everyone stopped to meet him."

Since rising to the occasion, Naki'o not only gets excited when he sees his prosthetic legs (like some dogs respond when the leash comes out), but he has become even more confident and even friendlier than he was before . . . and that's saying a lot. "He's so good with all kinds of people—children, elderly—and with other animals. I know it's because of what he's gone through."

His original prosthetics have been tweaked and reworked over time for an even better fit. And Christie selected a very special design to decorate them. "I picked the American flag. There were lots of options—camouflage and flowers and such. But I like the flag because I think of him as a hero and wanted to pay tribute to him and to the war-hero amputees who have struggled like he has. To say thank you."

Naki'o's ease and sweet temperament despite his ordeal have brought him much attention. "People see how much I've done for him, but really what's important is how much he's doing for others. How happy he is—how much joy and spirit and life he has—sets such a positive example. He's educating people that animals with serious disabilities can have a great quality of life."

And this "silly boy," as she calls him, seems to love showing off his newly found abilities. He's participated in an agility course—through tunnels, up

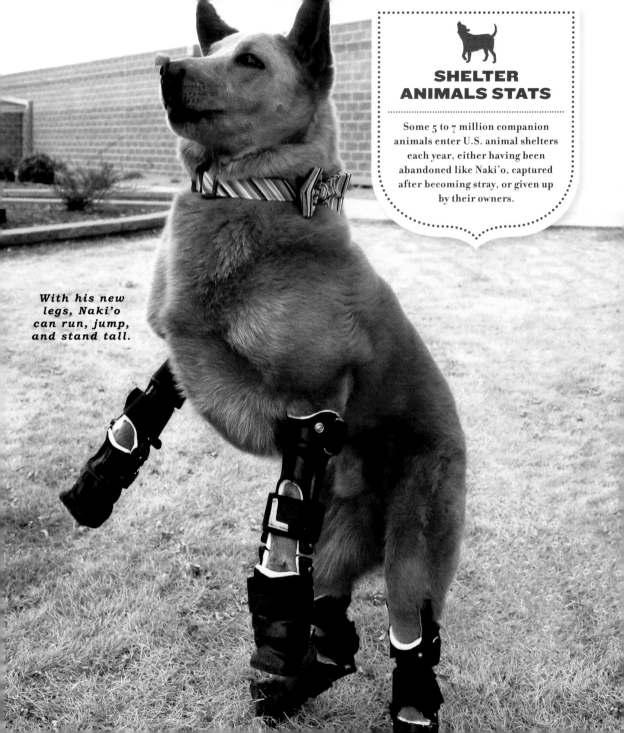

With his new legs, Naki'o can run, jump, and stand tall.

A-frames, between poles. "If anyone doubted he could do it, he certainly showed them!" Christie says with pride. She's taken him to rallies for disabled pets and to visit kids with disabilities. And most important, he inspired Christie to found a rescue organization in his name. Through Naki'o's Underdog Rescue, in Colorado Springs, Christie has been helping dogs and cats with disabilities to find loving homes. She's even had a few come in from overseas.

"We may not be able to assist animals in huge volume, but the few disabled animals we can help are worth it all," Christie says.

Meanwhile, Naki'o, unaware of the hero within him, keeps kicking up those feet and making people smile, bringing a little bit of magic wherever his new legs carry him.

All smiles during
physical therapy.

A Rabbit's Sixth Sense

SIMON STEGGALL NEARLY DROWNED WHEN HE WAS TWO years old. A neighbor had a pond surrounded by garden gnomes, and the little boy liked a particular gnome so much that when it toppled into the water while he was hugging it, he didn't let go. His mother, alerted by Simon's brother, pulled the boy out and revived him. His childhood continued apace. That was the first time Simon was very, very lucky.

Simon is now fifty-one, and lives in Colchester, the oldest town in England. He has Type 1 diabetes, diagnosed at age four. He manages his disease pretty well. He's a healthy man, riding horses, kayaking, and working full-time for British Telecom. He's been with the same employer for twenty-six years, and for a time

Dory's fuss drew attention to Simon's diabetic coma.

his work was extremely physical. As a telephone engineer, he climbed poles all day, sometimes up and down several times, which left him exhausted and sore, wanting nothing more than to sit in a comfortable chair and do nothing at all in the evenings. Except maybe pet Dory.

Dory (Simon borrowed the name from the film *Finding Nemo*) was a Flemish Giant rabbit, a breed known for its impressive stature. (In 2009, one named Benny, vying for the title of world's longest rabbit, grew to 2.6 feet long on about 60 pounds of food per week.) "Full-grown Dory weighed about one and three-quarters stone (nearly twenty-five pounds)! When she sat in your lap, she fully enveloped it." He'd had cats and dogs before, "but there's nothing quite like having a massive rabbit lying across you," he says. "It was lovely."

And she wasn't just a giant with sky-high ears: Dory also had a huge heart. The rabbit seemed to adore Simon; she'd cuddle up and rub her jaw against him, a marking behavior that translates to "you're mine." She was also voracious. He and his then wife, Victoria, would feed her cabbage and dried food, but she'd go outside and continue to feast on whatever greens she could find: dandelions, milkweed, and flowers. "She just grew and grew," Simon says.

So, the huge rabbit and Simon got along splendidly. And that relationship, it turned out, was paramount to the man's survival.

Back in January 2004, after one of those particularly tiring days of shimmying up and down telephone poles, Simon dragged himself home from the job, took off his soiled work clothes, and plopped into a comfortable chair. Flipping on the TV, he settled in for an evening of relaxation, to let his weary body recover.

Victoria noticed that Simon had dozed off in his chair. Meanwhile, Dory, yearning for the softness of Simon's lap, made her move, climbing to her favorite seat to stretch out. As a house rabbit, she was allowed certain privileges, but Victoria didn't like her on the furniture and told her to get down.

Now came Simon's second bout of luck. The rabbit ignored Victoria's order and began to act strangely. Rather than draping herself over Simon's legs, she put her giant paws against his chest and started scratching as if digging a hole—not roughly but enough to get Victoria's attention. "Victoria told me later that

Dory had made a terrible fuss, seeming very upset," Simon says. "She kept pawing at me, like she was trying to wake me up, until Victoria came over to see what was wrong."

Victoria, an ambulance driver by training, then realized Simon wasn't napping but instead had fallen into a diabetic coma—an extremely dangerous state. She moved fast to check Simon's blood sugar and get paramedics to the house.

"All I remember after sitting down to watch TV," Simon says, "is waking up on the floor with paramedics over me calling my name." The team revived Simon and treated him, leaving him at home to fully recover. "I was feeling quite confused—it was a pretty rough couple of hours afterward," he says. "Then I heard about what Dory had done. I knew right away that if she hadn't acted the way she did, I could easily have died."

He's not sure how to explain Dory's actions. "I don't know if the body smells different when your sugar is low—as it does when it's high—but maybe Dory was clued in by scent," Simon says. He recalls that he once had a dog who, when Simon had low blood sugar, would slink by him, not wanting to get close, perhaps sensing the change.

"But also, normally when Dory would sit on me I would stroke her fur and scratch her ears. Maybe she was upset that I wasn't touching her, so she pawed me to ask me what was going on, why I wasn't making a fuss over her."

Simon says Dory quickly became a local celebrity and a

media darling. "And I treated her like royalty," he says. "We bought fancy savoy cabbage for her and other special food treats. We really spoiled her."

"If it weren't for Dory, things could have ended horribly that day," he says. "She was a true hero. A life saver."

The ability some animals have to smell or sense human disease could be tapped by doctors in the future. Researchers have already shown that dogs, in particular, can smell a variety of cancers. Maybe someday Fido will come sniffing during your physical exams, or it could even be a rabbit like Dory wriggling its nose to your unique scent, perhaps even saving your life.

★

AWARDS & HONORS

Dory was awarded an honorary membership in the British Rabbit Council, the first nonhuman to be granted this status.

Mr. and Mrs. Spock.

The Cooperative Cranes

MR. AND MRS. SPOCK THROW THEIR HEADS BACK, beaks to the sky, and sound off. Loudly. They're both adorned in brown-mottled gray feathers and they have red masks across their tangerine eyes. Their duet is seamless: two quick trumpets from her in reply to each toot from him. They're letting me know they aren't happy that I'm this close to them. I step back a bit from the fence that separates us and they go quiet. They've got their eyes on me, though. Unless I'm going to feed them, my visit is unwelcome.

This mated pair of sandhill cranes, the male of which has little pointy tufts extending up from his ears (thus the name "Spock"), lives at the Patuxent Wildlife Research Center in Laurel,

A whooping crane chick.

Maryland. They're part of a conservation effort aimed at an endangered cousin of theirs, the snow-white whooping crane. Sandhills aren't in decline. They've adapted well to human activity at the edges of their habitat and their populations are doing well. But the whooping cranes are struggling, their numbers decimated by hunting and habitat loss. In the 1930s, just fifteen adult whoopers remained in the wild. Scientists are committed to saving them, and have made great strides. Part of that success they owe to sandhill cranes.

Patuxent has been breeding whooping cranes in captivity since the 1960s and releasing birds into wild populations in Louisiana and Wisconsin. Using crane costumes and hand puppets that look like crane heads, the scientists raise the birds as naturally as possible, even teaching them how to migrate by following ultralight aircraft as they would follow an adult bird. The program has been terrific in many ways, but it has failed in one important one. The introduced birds just won't sit on their eggs long enough to hatch them. The scientists aren't yet sure why. (It may have to do with black flies driving them out of the nests, but more studies are needed to be sure.)

Until the birds in the wild consistently manage to hatch chicks, scientists need to keep making whooping cranes. And this is where the sandhill cranes perform some very important jobs. First, they are guinea pigs for any new project. Because whoopers are so valuable, scientists test ideas and equipment on the sandhills before trying them out on the endangered birds. For example, the captive breeding techniques, including the design of the costumes and hand puppets, and the ultralight migration effort, were developed with sandhills first. So was a vaccine that is now given to all whoopers to protect them from West Nile virus. Sandhills are also "royal tasters" for any new foods or vitamins. And most important, they are sit-in whooper crane egg warmers.

Cranes generally lay two eggs at a time (a "clutch"). If you take the eggs away, the parents will quickly lay more. So, when the endangered whoopers lay eggs, the scientists carefully remove them from the nest and tuck them under nesting sandhill cranes. The whoopers then lay another pair of eggs and the scientists repeat the sneaky maneuver. Typically, they can get three extra clutches of eggs per female per season. And that means many more cranes to help boost the wild populations.

Incubators—the kind you plug in—do a good job with the eggs, but live cranes are more attentive. Mr. and Mrs. Spock are two of Patuxent's most effective surrogates, along with a little gal named

Steve (above) incubates; the Spocks (left) await new eggs.

Steve (after a former intern). It felt like the hottest day of the year when John French, a wildlife toxicologist who heads up the crane projects, and Brian Clauss, a biological technician, showed me around some of the 200 acres of crane pens, row upon row of stately, noisy birds. Sandhill Steve looked an awful lot like Mr. and Mrs. Spock, but I was assured that these birds, though similar in appearance, have their own personalities. And apparently, not every sandhill is a suitable surrogate.

With the Spocks, John said, "You can give 'em anything and they'll sit on it." And Steve is similarly easygoing. (She was less annoyed by my being outside her cage than most of the others.) But some cranes are pickier. They somehow realize the eggs aren't theirs—whooper eggs are bigger—and refuse to stay put. Or they might crack the eggs. Or they might not turn the eggs enough with their beaks, a behavior that helps the young develop properly. The crane scientists look at the traits of each sandhill pair and rate them. "We have some fifty pairs that are surrogates in training," French says. "The best ones will perform an essential service." (Typically males and females take turns incubating eggs, though singles like Steve can be capable sitters.)

CRANE DANCING

All species of cranes dance, with graceful moves that include bowing and wing flapping, jumping, and stick or grass tossing. Dancing is often about mating, but it also contributes to the birds' motor development, thwarts aggression, relieves tension, and strengthens pair bonds.

Essential, yes. And when the goal is no less than saving a species from extinction, I'd say heroic. Consider that little Steve has been a surrogate for fifteen years, incubating two to three clutches a year. I'm no math whiz, but that adds up to a lot of birds that might otherwise not have been. With the whooping crane total population only in the hundreds, that's a pretty impressive contribution. So a standing ovation for sandhill cranes—the Spocks, little Steve, and many others—as they help to keep the whooper on the wing.

Thanks to two Maremma sheepdogs, Middle Island's little penguin population has grown from seven to 200.

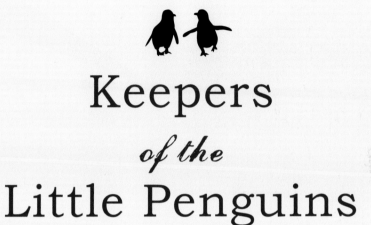

Keepers
of the
Little Penguins

ON THE SEA-BEATEN COASTS OF SOUTHERN **A**USTRALIA and New Zealand lives the smallest penguin on Earth. It is appropriately called the little penguin (or, delightfully, the fairy penguin), and it is a gem of a bird, tidily dressed in a hooded cape of blue, with a white belly and hazel eyes.

A breeding colony of these unique birds lives on Middle Island, a chunk of rock off Victoria, Australia, near the city of Warrnambool. At sunrise, the penguins go to sea to catch and eat fish, squid, and other small swimmers, and come back onto shore at dark. They usually forage for food in shallow water but some-times dive as deep as 65 feet. Life is good in their Middle Island habitat, with its food-rich waters and perfect sites for egg-laying

Eudy and Tula on fox patrol.

burrows. Except there's one big problem. During November and December, at low tide, the water becomes so shallow that foxes can slink over from the mainland on a bridge of sand. (They'll even swim over, if they have to, but they prefer to keep their furry selves dry.) Foxes love penguins, but not in the nice way. To them, the little birds are tasty morsels, easily hunted down. At one time, the foxes were so thorough in their harvest that the Middle Island penguin population, which before the year 2000 had been around 600 birds, declined to just seven animals in 2005.

I should mention that despite the slaughter on Middle

Island, little penguins aren't an endangered species; they're not even considered threatened. Although domestic cats and dogs have taken out many mainland colonies in their native Australia and New Zealand, they are still plentiful on the coasts and islands. There are probably about a million of them throughout their range. But this particular group was clearly in big trouble. And mainland residents are attached to Middle Island's penguins. The birds are a part of the local landscape and culture, so folks wanted to bring the population back.

PROTECTING THE LITTLE PENGUINS

In a dramatic move, the Australian parks service once hired professional snipers to defend the besieged colony of little penguins.

City Council staff tried everything to pick off the offending foxes, from baiting to fumigating the island to playing sniper. But none was a long-term solution. So in 2006, the council, the Warrnambool Coastcare Landcare Group, and community volunteers decided to unite and enlist a special guarding

Lovely little fairies.

force. They chose the burly and beautiful Maremma sheepdog to do the job, in an effort called the Middle Island Maremma Project. Sheepdogs are certainly excellent protectors of livestock, and as one chicken farmer put it, "to dogs, penguins are only chooks [slang for chickens] in dinner suits." Still, it was an experiment.

Happily, it worked beautifully. The Maremmas turned out to be perfect penguin protectors. From the beginning, foxes were sent packing and the penguin numbers slowly began to rise. Less than a decade later, the population is estimated to be nearing 200, a big jump from seven. The current heroes to the penguins are a pair of young Maremmas, Eudy and Tula, who live and work on the island from September into April. Eudy is a bit of a loner—happy to check people out but then go about her business. Tula is the social one, the tail wagger, always happy to see you. They've bonded with the land, the volunteers and staff, the birds, and each other. And they take their job very seriously, patroling the island each morning to look for and drive out any intruders, then keeping watch throughout the day and night—snoozing on and off when all is quiet.

"One reason we picked this breed is that they think before they act," explains Paul Hartrick from the Warrnambool City Council. "Ordinary domestic dogs just bark their heads off. But these animals only bark if another dog or a fox gets too close and becomes an actual threat. That's when they act." If a fox is near, the dogs will herd the penguins together and stand between them and the predator, he says. "And if the fox moves in, then they'll chase."

To help this program to thrive, the island has been closed to the public since 2006 and will remain that way for the forseeable future. The community has given this idea its blessing, realizing that for these beloved penguins to keep reproducing successfully, they need some privacy. Having people scrambling over the rocks and beaches snapping photos could interfere with this essential behavior. Meanwhile, not wanting to lock the public out entirely, the Warrnambool City Council runs tours every summer to give people a glimpse of the little penguins and the Maremmas that protect them.

These dogs probably don't realize they are providing such a heroic service, of course. But says Paul, "They dedicate their lives to protecting these penguins, and they really seem to enjoy their role."

On behalf of the little fairies, a big thanks to their furry protectors!

The Mine-Sniffing Rats

ARARAT WAS ALWAYS A FRIENDLY GUY, CALM UNDER pressure, gentle with others, and talented at his job. He was also a quick learner who aced all his tests. Every day, putting his talents to work, he risked his life to help people. But Ararat was no typical soldier. At 6 pounds, with big ears, a long, whiskered nose, and a scantily haired tail, Ararat was a warrior with the body and mind of a rodent.

In the aftermath of wars around the world, African pouched rats like Ararat (*Cricetomys gambianus*)—your basic alley rats on steroids—are unlikely heroes.

War is always tragic. And often, even after quiet settles over battle-weary regions, hidden dangers lie in wait. In countries like

Sniffer rats have helped clear thousands of acres of land mines.

Mozambique and Angola in Africa, where wars drag on for decades, landscapes remain sullied with land mines—explosives hidden underground that are triggered when someone or something steps on them. Every month, people step on mines and are injured or killed. The same goes on in more than sixty other countries around the world. So, even when peace comes, wars continue to devastate.

APOPO (which stands for *Anti-Persoonsmijnen Ontmijnende Product Ontwikkeling*) is a Belgian organization based in Tanzania, eastern Africa, that seeks ways to disarm and get rid of land mines as safely as possible. And since 1996, their staff has been working with these intelligent African rats, training them to sniff out explosives the way dogs in the United States sniff out drugs and bad guys.

With their sensitive noses so close to the ground, rats can pick up the vapor given off by explosive material (TNT), and they can be easily trained to let a trainer know when they smell it. Unlike a human de-miner, the cat-size workers aren't heavy enough to set off the mines when they skitter across them. Plus, they're long-lived, easy to breed and take care of, and they don't mind being carried around from place to place.

The captive-bred African rats may be hard for an outsider to tell apart, but no two are truly alike. They're much like kids, and each has its own personality. "Some are very energetic, constantly moving and running about," says Timothy Edwards, APOPO's head of training and research, "while others are more relaxed, like Ararat. A few of the rats are very vocal, happily squeaking when they are about to be fed, while they are being handled, and sometimes while they are working."

Mine detection—both training and the real thing—often goes on under the hot sun, so trainers massage sun-blocking lotion into the rats' naked ears and tails before they go into the field. In training, the animals wear a harness attached to a cord that helps guide them up and back in the area to be cleared. For bits of banana (and the sound of a clicker) as reward, they learn to thoroughly sniff a section of land and to signal, by scratching the ground, when they smell the key ingredient. Once a rat locates and signals a finding, human de-miners move in with metal detectors and excavation tools to do the dangerous work of digging up the mine and disarming it.

Ararat was the first "jackpot" rat, according to Abdullah Ramadhani, the training manager at APOPO's headquarters in Tanzania. "It was still the early days, when we weren't sure how

A successful find and (next page) a reward!

accurate these rats could be. He was the first rat that made no errors in his final test. He hit all of the mines with no false indications" (meaning he didn't mistakenly signal mines that weren't there). Ararat showed the trainers just what these animals were capable of doing—how heroic they could someday be. Now APOPO has around 200 mine-smelling rats in training or actually working somewhere in the world, plus one hundred breeders in the process of adding to the force.

Once the rats know their jobs, they are shipped to where they're most needed—Mozambique, Angola, and

SNIFFER RATS

Trainers at APOPO first tried using wild-caught rats as sniffers, since they are already well adapted to the harsh environments in which they'd be working. But they found it better to breed the rats themselves, exposing them to key odors very early in life.

The rats can detect the smell of TNT.

in the future Cambodia—to join mine-detecting teams. From then on, they are up before the sun and trucked to sites that need their noses. They spend 40-minute stints sniffing over lands suspected of being pocked with explosives—no longer rewarded for each discovery but still content to do the work. After their morning runs, they munch on peanuts, pieces of banana, and nutritional pellets back in their cages before curling up for some much-deserved naps.

How heroic have the mine-sniffing rats been so far? Timothy says: "If you look at the number of land mines found by the rats, you might think that they play a relatively small role in mine detection. But if you look at the amount of space cleared, you get a completely different message." By the end of a four-year project in Mozambique, for example, the rats had helped clear and return some 8 million square meters of land to the people of Mozambique. (That's around 2,000 acres, more than twice the size of New York's Central Park.) During that effort, they'd pointed their noses at some 3,000 land mines plus a host of other dangerous weapons.

And there's more. The rat noses aren't just prepped to find mines. The same species, researchers have found, is also sensitive to the scent of tuberculosis (TB), a deadly bacterial disease, and can be trained to find that, too. In labs in developing countries, another batch of APOPO's trained rats run their noses over rows of test tubes, and reveal TB-infected samples from people whose disease was overlooked by technicians using a microscope. That turns out to be a lot of people! As an example, in one region in sub-Saharan Africa, sniffer rats identified 4,722 people who were TB-positive and needed treatment. Those people hadn't been getting care before because no one knew they were sick. Timothy says, "When you consider that each person with active TB can infect ten to fifteen others each year," and that one rat can evaluate in 10 minutes more samples than a technician can do in a full day, "that is a major accomplishment."

Which is why APOPO's animals are known as HeroRATS. "When I think of a hero, I think of someone who does dangerous or difficult work to help others without asking for much in return," says Timothy. "I think that our rats fit this description perfectly." Between sniffing countless samples to help combat TB and doing the tedious (and risky) mine-detecting runs under the fierce African sun, they certainly deserve their nickname, he says. And in perfect hero form, the animals have modest needs when the job is done. "All they ask in return," he says, "is a bite of banana, a few peanuts, a clay pot to sleep in, and a stick to gnaw."

The Sheep *Who* Rammed Cancer

EMMA TURNER WASN'T A SHEEP PERSON. SHE DIDN'T grow up with them, didn't visit the sheep farm that her husband's great-aunt and -uncle ran, and didn't really know much about them. "I'm from West London," she explains.

But some twenty years ago, she and husband David Foster moved to Wiltshire, in the southwest of England, where they began keeping horses. And horses are fussy about itchy weeds growing around their legs, she says, "so it's useful to have a few sheep to take the grass down a bit." They selected a local breed that was relatively rare, the Cotswold sheep.

Alfie is a sheep that almost wasn't. First, his breed almost disappeared in the 1960s, long before he was born. Only because of the passionate efforts of breeders did the Cotswold avoid fading into obscurity. And second, Alfie was born to a very sick ewe and had a difficult birth that could easily have killed him. "Alfie was born the second lambing we did," Emma recalls of the now 120-kilo (264-pound) male. His mum, Mazy, passed away before Alfie reached a week old. "The lamb was starved of oxygen. He ended up with some wonky movements—a shambling walk and jerky trot. He was also generally unwell for the first eighteen months. We saved him over and over again."

Perhaps because of his fight for survival, she says, "I always liked him. He was friendly. He'd been bottle-fed after his mum died, and stayed in a kitchen under a heat lamp, so he was used to people. And over time, he became very charismatic. He's now a schmoozer. Because his body doesn't always obey him, he uses his brain to cleverly get what he wants." A big, intelligent, and curious

When Alfie started acting strangely, Emma knew something was wrong.

beast, he's also moody, she says, "a typical Cotswold. They all have that side."

But one thing about Alfie: He's predictable around his owners. Emma knows him well and is rarely surprised by his behavior. So the day he started acting out, she had to wonder what was going on.

"It was October 2010, and October is prep time when you raise sheep," Emma says. "We get all the sheep ready to breed, check all the feet and teeth, and make sure everyone is healthy. Alfie was in a funny mood. Normally, he's very good at picking up his feet, leaning against the wall, letting us check him over. But on that day, he went a bit bonkers."

It took three people to wrestle Alfie into a workable position, sitting so that his back was leaning against Emma's body. "His head was against the top of my chest," she says. "And suddenly he started butting his head backward, over and over, smashing against me. It was really painful—he kept hitting the same spot. Then, he flounced away. It was all so out of character. I even thought about ringing the vet, he was acting so strangely."

Alfie seemed normal the next day, but Emma had terrible bruising where the sheep's head had made repeated contact. And then, after a few days, Emma noticed something sinister: "a small hard lump right in the middle of the bruise on my right breast. It was right in the center, and I only noticed it because of the trauma there." She went to her doctor, had a variety of scans and

If Alfie (top) didn't act when he did, Emma's cancer would have spread very quickly.

a biopsy, and finally got that scary news that the lump was indeed cancer. An aggressive type.

"Very definitely, at that point I was thinking about Alfie. He was on everyone's mind at the hospital, as well. They were completely convinced Alfie did it on purpose. Even my surgeon thought so. You hear about dogs sniffing out cancer in their owners, so why not a sheep?"

Emma wasn't sure what to think. "But I was certainly aware that Alfie had done me a very good turn," she says. Regardless of how it was revealed, the cancer had to be treated quickly.

Of course no one knows whether Alfie sensed something was wrong with Emma or was just having a bad day when he flailed about and struck her chest. Either way, "I owe him my life," Emma says. He led her to the first tumor, and it turned out she had more cancer than the doctor expected, set to run wild into her lymph nodes. "He saved my life and, my surgeon says, did so at exactly the right time." If that cancer had had a little more time to spread, the doc says, it would have gone quite fast and this story would have a much less happy ending.

Alfie also helped Emma's husband during the worst of Emma's illness. "The sheep was a terrific comfort to him," Emma says, "as he was to me. I still go tell him my problems—he's a good listener." In appreciation, the family treats Alfie very well, giving him birthday parties and special treats and massages for his achy joints, and they regularly update his Facebook page (yes, he has one!) with his funny antics. A friend of Emma's even wrote a song for him.

COTSWOLD COMEBACK

Once extremely rare, these beautiful sheep are now popular with spinners. The animals can yield 15 pounds of wool per shearing.

"Maybe it was just chance," says Emma, now two years cancer-free and feeling well. "But his behavior that day was so out of character for him, and he hasn't done anything like that since. He's remarkable, and I wouldn't put it past him . . . he certainly could have known."

Regardless, let's add Alfie to the ever-growing list of wonderfully unlikely heroes.

"I owe him my life," Emma says.

References

Balas, M. "Oregon City Hero Cat That Rescued Soldier to Be Honored by ASPCA." *Oregonian* (Portland, OR), November 11, 2013.

Bat Conservation International. "The Tale of the Flying Fox Midwife." *BATS* magazine 13 (2), Summer 1995.

BBC News. "Rabbit Saves Diabetic from Coma." (January 29, 2004): news.bbc.co.uk/2/hi/uk_news/England/cambridgeshire/3441337.stm.

BBC News. "Skippy to the Rescue." (September 22, 2003): news.bbc.co.uk/2/hi/asia-pacific/3127814.stm.

Bhanoo, S. N. "Four-Legged Assistants Sniff Out Wildlife Data." *New York Times*, January 14, 2011.

Bideawee. "A Most Unlikely Cat Hero." (2013, Studio One Networks): bideawee.org/S1-TCC-Blog-oklahoma_cat_hero-426.

Bohn, K. M., C. F. Moss, and G. S. Wilkinson. "Pup Guarding by Greater Spear-Nosed Bats." *Behavioral Ecology and Sociobiology* (June 10, 2009): link.springer.com/article/10.1007%2Fs00265-009-0776-8/.

Bonsper, P. "Dan & Shadow: The Sky's the Limit." *Coastal Canine*, Fall 2013.

Breuning, L. G. "The Myth of Animal Altruism." *Psychology Today*, May 24, 2011.

Britannica.com. African Pouched Rat. britannica.com/EBchecked/topic/472950/African-pounched-rat#toc226067.

Britannica.com. Manawatu River. britannica.com/EBchecked/topic/361352/Manawatu-River.

Britannica.com. Syrinx. britannica.com/EBchecked/topic/579069/syrinx.

CBS Chicago. "15 Years Ago Today: Gorilla Rescues Boy Who Fell in Ape Pit." (August 16, 2011): chicago/cbslocal.com.

Centre National de la Recherche Scientifique. "Why Are Animals Altruistic?" *Science Daily* (April 5, 2006): sciencedaily.com/releases/2006/04/060404201741.htm.

Chakraborty, Debajyoti. "Elephant Pulls Down House in Bengal, Then Rescues 10-Month-Old Baby Trapped Under Debris." (March 12, 2014): timesofindia.indiatimes.com/india/Elephant-pulls-down-house-in-Bengal-then-rescues-10-month-old-baby-trapped-under-debris/articleshow/31860512.cms.

Chapman, Paul. "Swimming Cow Saves Farmer's Wife." *Telegraph* (New Zealand) (February 18, 2004): telegraph.co.uk/news/worldnews/australiaandthepacific/newzealand/1454679.

Corpsman.com. "Veterans Day 2010." corpsman.com/2010/11/in-war-there-are-no-unwounded-soldiers-jose-narosky-veterans-day-2010/#Scene_1.

Cox, C., et al. "Rats for Demining: An Overview of the APOPO Program." apopo.org/images/publications.

Defenders of Wildlife. "Basic Facts About Sea Otters." (2013): defenders.org/sea-otter/basic-facts.

De Waal, F. "Moral Behavior in Animals," TED talk, April 10, 2012. ted.com/speakers/frans_de_waal.

Encyclopedia of New Zealand 1966. "Manawatu River." teara.govt.nz/en/1996/manawatu-river.

Fried, J. "A Few Short of 9 Lives, but Still Much Beloved." *New York Times*, March 4, 2001.

The Guardian. "Giant Rats Put Noses to Work on Mozambique's Landmines." (January 22, 2014): theguardian.com/global-development/.

Hay's Daily News. "KVMA Present Pet of the Year Awards." (June 17, 2013): hdnews.net/news/Pet061813.

Horner, V., et al. "Spontaneous Prosocial Choice by Chimpanzees." *Proceedings of the National Academy of Sciences* 108 (13), August 16, 2011.

Horsetalk. "Heroic Horse Saves Woman from Death by Cow." horsetalk.co.nz/archives/2007/08/110.shtml#axzz2Uhetja6v.

Huffington Post. "Hero Parrot 'Willie' Saves Choking Girl." huffingtonpost.com/2009/03/hero-parrot-willie-saves-_n_178586.html.

Huffington Post. "Lioness Attacks Crocodile to Protect Pride." huffingtonpost.com/2012/07/25/lioness-fends-off-alliga_n_1701939.html.

Kumaran, C. "The Floods of February 2004." *Impact* 17, March 2004.

Kunz, T. H., et al. "Allomaternal Care: Helper-Assisted Birth in the Rodrigues Fruit Bat, *Pteropus rodricensis*." *Journal of Zoology London* 232, 691–700, 1994.

LAist. "Heroic Llama Saves Flock of Sheep from Cajon Pass Brush Fire." laist.com/2011/09/12/heroic_llama_saves_flock_of_sheep.php.

Laskow, S. "Surrogate-Mom Housecat Gives Birth to Endangered Kitten." Grist.org, March 14, 2012.

Mahoney, A., et al. "Mine Detection Rats: Effects of Repeated Extinction on Detection Accuracy." (Fall 2012): jmu.edu/cisr/journal/16.3/rd/mahoney.shtml.

Mail Online. "Elk and Safety: Zookeepers Stunned as Moose Rescues Drowning Marmot from Watery Death." (July 1, 2011): dailymail.co.uk/news/article-2009820/.

Metro. "The helpful hippo that rescues helpless animals." metro.co.uk/2010/11/10/577284.

Monterey Bay Aquarium Institute. "Sea Otter Research and Conservation at the Monterey Bay Aquarium" (seminar): mbari.org/seminars/2000/Fall2000/dec06_johnson.html.

Naeger, N., et al. "Altruistic Behaviour by Egg-Laying Worker Honeybees." *Current Biology*, August 2013.

No Feather Left Behind Avian Rescue. "How Do Birds Talk Without Vocal Chords?" birdyrevolution.blogspot.com/2011/01/how-do-birds-talk.html.

O'Beollain, P. "Partially Paralyzed Former Shelter Rabbit Helps Pediatric Patients." (April 25, 2010): examiner.com/article/.

Olsen, G. H., et al. "Pathogenicity of West Nile Virus and Response to Vaccination in Sandhill Cranes (*Grus Canadensis*) Using a Killed Vaccine." *Journal of Zoo and Wildlife Medicine* 40 (2): 263–271 (2009): bioone.org/doi/abs/10.1638/2008-0017.1.

Olson, Y. S. "Dog's Friendship Saves Veteran's Life." mysuburbanlife.com: gurneesuburbanlife.com/2013/05/22/dogs-friendship-saves-veterans-life/ayfetgx.

Oskin, B. "Sheepdogs Save Australia's Endangered Penguins." (June 2, 2013): livescience.com/37097-dogs-protect-endangered-penguins.html.

Parker, M. "Wildlife Detection Dogs." The Wildlife Society, May 26, 2011.

PBS Nature. "Saving Otter 501" 2013: pbs.org/wnet/nature/episodes/saving-otter-501.

Penguin Foundation. "About Little Penguins" penguinfoundation.org.au/about-little-penguins.

Phys.org. "New Research Provides Evolutionary Snapshot of Surprisingly Altruistic Bees": phys.org/news/2013-08-evolutionary-snapshot-surprisingly-altruistic-bees.html#jCp.

Plotnik, J. M., and Frans B. M. de Waal. "Asian Elephants (*Elephas maximus*) Reassure Others in Distress." *PeerJ* 2 (278) (February 2014): peerj.com/articles/278.

Poling, A., et al. "Two strategies for landmine detection by giant pouched rats." *Journal of ERW and Mine Action* (Spring 2010): jmu.edu/cisr/journal/14.1/R_D/poling.shtml.

Poling, A., et al. "Using Trained Pouched Rats to Detect Landmines: Another Victory for Operant Conditioning." *Journal of Applied Behavioral Analysis* (Summer 2011): ncbi.nlm .nih.gov/pmc/articles/PMC3120071.

Richard, M. G. "Sheepdog 'Bodyguards' Protect Endangered Penguins from Foxes, Saving Them from Extinction." *Treehugger.com* (June 3, 2013): treehugger.com/natural -sciences/sheepdog-bodyguard-protect-endangered-penguins-foxes-australia.html.

Rural Delivery. "Riley's Dairy." (April 3, 2010): ruraldelivery.net.nz/2010/04/rileys-dairy/.

Salazar, J. "Chimp Test Shows Planet of Altruistic Apes." EarthSky (August 10, 2011): earthsky.org/human-world/.

Stokes, Paul. "Seal Swims to Rescue of Drowning Dog." *Telegraph* (New Zealand) (June 20, 2002): telegraph.co.uk/news/uknews/1397813/seal-swims-to-rescue-of-drowning-dog .html.

Thometz, N. M. et al. "Energetic demands of immature sea otters from birth to weaning: implications for maternal costs, reproductive behavior and population-level trends," *Journal of Experimental Biology* (June 15, 2014) 217, 2053–2061.

U.S. Geological Survey. "The Whooping Crane: Return from the Brink of Extinction." whoopers.usgs.gov/publications/CraneInfoSheet_4pp.pdf.

Wallace, R. "Paralyzed Bunny Helps Children Overcome Their Own Disabilities." *Zootoo* (March 26, 2010): zootoo.com/petnews/paralyzed-bunny-helps-children -overcome-their-own-disabilities-1554.

White, Tracie. "For Elephants, Deciding to Leave the Watering Hole Demands Conversation, Study Shows." (October 2, 2012): med.stanford.edu/ism/2012/october/elephant.html# sthash.k5MBDWkX.dpuf.

World Wildlife Fund. "Western Lowland Gorilla." worldwildlife.org/species/western -lowland-gorilla.

WZZM13. "Comstock Park Woman Gets Attention for Service Goat." May 23, 2013: wzzm13 .com/news/article/257388/14/Comstock-Park-woman-gets-attention-for-service-goat.

Yahoo News. "Dolphins Saved My Life: Woman Says." (March 5, 2013): au.news.yahoo.com/ odd/a/-/odd/16301522/dolphins-saved-my-life-woman.

Yang, S. "Wildlife Biologists Put Dogs' Scat-Sniffing Talents to Good Use." newscenter .berkeley.edu/2011/01/11/dogs/.

Yerkes National Primate Research Center, Emory University. "Chimpanzees Are Spontaneously Generous After All." (August 8, 2011): yerkes.emory.edu/about/news/ developmental_cognitive_neuroscience/chimpanzees_generous.html.

ADDITIONAL WEB SOURCES

Alley Cat Allies: alleycat.org

British Rabbit Council: thebrc.org

Center for Orthotics Design: centerfororthoticsdesign.com/isocentric_rgo/index.html

International Union for Conservation of Nature Red List of Threatened Species: iucnredlist. org/details/8542/0

Leonberger Club of America: leonbergerclubofamerica.info
Little Penguin: en.wikipedia.org.wiki.Little_Penguin
Middle Island: en.wikipedia.org/wiki/Middle_Island_ (Warrnambool)
Middle Island Maremma Project: warrnambool.vic.gov.au/index.php?q=node/943
Mountain Peaks Therapy Llamas & Alpacas: rojothellama.com
QuakerParrots.com: quakerparrots.com/quaker-parrot-faq
Tanzania National Parks: tanzaniaparks.com/news/migration.html

Acknowledgments

As always, I'm extremely grateful to the animal lovers who shared their wonderful stories with me. Without them, these pages would be blank.

Thanks to my affectionate husband, John, for sharing my highs, keeping me laughing, and suffering (mostly with grace) the slings of my writing process. Hugs also to father Martin, step-dad Mark, brother Adam, and Aunt Judy for the love and support, always. I'm grateful to my in-laws, Lorie, Glenn, Lenora, and Ross, for encouragement, nourishment, wine, and family love.

Special appreciation goes to my loyal and talented researcher Kate Horowitz for sticking with me for another round, and deep thanks to friend and wordsmith extraordinaire Lynne Warren for so many things. A toast also to my fabulous women friends, who keep me as close to sane as possible: You know who you are!

Thanks to gentle listener Margaret Storey for fortifying me, and to my agent, Suzanne Gluck, for her stellar advice and no-nonsense attitude. Thanks, too, to So-Young Lee for her work on translations. To Gerald Carter, thanks for patient explanations of complex ideas and for a seat in the bat cave.

I'm grateful to the kids in my life for inspiring me to stay young and keeping me hopeful: Kate, Will, Elliott, and Jasper, plus Cree, Hannah, P. G., Abigael, and Theo. You are terrific people and I'm happy to know you.

Dogs Waits and Monk, thanks for your sweet (slightly smelly) company and for warming my feet all winter long. And a big welcome to new dog Geddy, my latest muse. Let the canine chaos continue.

Finally, a huge heartfelt thanks to my Workman "family"—Krestyna Lypen for terrific editing and sound ideas, Melissa Lucier for yet another heroic photo effort, Maggie Gleason and Chloe Puton for enthusiastic publicity, Ariana Abud for the inspired design work, Tae Won Yu for the sweet illustrations on the story pages, Beth Levy for taking care of all the little details, and Sam O'Brien for helping me toward the big finish. And I'd be remiss if I didn't once again recognize Raquel Jaramillo for believing in me in the first place.

Jennifer S. Holland

Photo Credits

Front cover and title page composite: Naki'o by Rick Wilking/Reuters; background grass by Siede Preis/Getty Images.

Back cover spots: James Weis/BNPS (left), George Karbus Photography/Getty Images (right).

Interior photographs: Courtesy of Alyn Hospital: p. 146, p. 148; Associated Press: p. 48, p. 51 (top and bottom); Barcroft/Landov: p. 75, p. 76; Maarten Boersema: p. 226, p. 231; Christy Bogner: pp. 84–88; Caters News Agency Ltd: p. 116 (top right), p. 116 (middle right), p. 121; Julie Crawford/Central Oklahoma Humane Society: p. 83; Marty Davis: p. 137; Pia Dierickx: p. v (middle), pp. 152–159; Elyse Fair/Central Oklahoma Humane Society: p. 78; Fairfax Media New Zealand: p. 105, p. 106; courtesy of Nancy Fite: p. 122, p. 124, p. 126; David Forster and Emma Turner: pp. 234–239; Karyn Gitsham p. 108, p. 112; courtesy of Lori Gregory: p. 138; Dave Hamman: p. 188; Lon Hodge: p. v (top), p. 140, p. 142 (bottom), p. 143; Meagan Howard: p. 58; Sue Howes: p. 31; imageBROKER/Alamy Images: p. 196; George Karbus Photography/Getty Images: p. 28; Abdul Karim: pp. 40–44; Jesse Knott: pp. 172–176; Álvaro Laiz: p. 230; Murdo Macleod: p. 66, p. 69; Sara Manley: pp. 160–165; michaklootwijk/fotolia: p. 63; Middle Island Maremma Project: p. 220, p. 222, p. 223, p. 225; Mint Images/Getty Images: p. 195; courtesy of © Monterey Bay Aquarium, photo by Randy Wilder: p. iv, p. vi, p. 180, p. 182, p. 183, p. 184; Vic Neumann: p. 15, p. 33; Michael Nolan/Getty Images: p. 110; North Shore Animal League America: p. 37; Nuneaton & Warwickshire Wildlife Sanctuary/Peter Corns: p. ii, p. 116 (left), p. 116 (bottom); Scott Olson/Getty Images: p. 46; © Christie Pace: p. 201, p. 202, p. 207; Patuxent Wildlife Research Center USGS/Jane Chandler: p. 214, p. 218; Patuxant Wildlife Research Center USGS/Barbara Claus: p. 216; Photolibrary/Getty Images: p. 64; Siede Preis/Getty Images: p. 198 (background grass); Richard Rayner/North News and Pictures: p. 60; Rex USA: p. 72; Joy Rexroat: pp. 90–94; Tamara Reynolds Photography: p. 22, p. 25, p. 55, p. 57; courtesy of Kim Riley: p. 103 (cow in composite); Gary Rohde: pp. 128–131; Hugh Ryono: p. v (bottom), pp. 16–20; courtesy of Bruce Schumacher: pp. 96–99; Vlad Skibunov/Shutterstock: p.103 (grass in composite) Nancy Steele: p. 134; Simon Steggall: pp. 208–210; courtesy of Jeff Strout/Audubon Nature Institute: p. 192; Jim Urquhart/Reuters: pp. 166–170; James Weis/BNPS: p. 74; Karen Wellen: p. 36; Rick Wilking/Reuters: p. 198 (Naki'o), p. 205; Working Dogs for Conservation: p. 186, p. 189; Xiaoli Xu: p. 4, p. 142 (top); Taro Yamasaki/Time & Life Pictures/Getty Images: p. 34, p. 39; Chiba Yasuyoshi: p. 228, p. 232.